Jumpstart Snowflake

A Step-by-Step Guide to Modern Cloud Analytics

Second Edition

Dmitry Anoshin
Dmitry Foshin
Donna Strok

Apress®

Jumpstart Snowflake: A Step-by-Step Guide to Modern Cloud Analytics, Second Edition

Dmitry Anoshin
North Vancouver, BC, Canada

Dmitry Foshin
Arcozelo, Portugal

Donna Strok
Seattle, WA, USA

ISBN-13 (pbk): 979-8-8688-1532-4
https://doi.org/10.1007/979-8-8688-1533-1

ISBN-13 (electronic): 979-8-8688-1533-1

Copyright © 2025 by Dmitry Anoshin, Dmitry Foshin and Donna Strok

This work is subject to copyright. All rights are reserved by the Publisher, whether the whole or part of the material is concerned, specifically the rights of translation, reprinting, reuse of illustrations, recitation, broadcasting, reproduction on microfilms or in any other physical way, and transmission or information storage and retrieval, electronic adaptation, computer software, or by similar or dissimilar methodology now known or hereafter developed.

Trademarked names, logos, and images may appear in this book. Rather than use a trademark symbol with every occurrence of a trademarked name, logo, or image we use the names, logos, and images only in an editorial fashion and to the benefit of the trademark owner, with no intention of infringement of the trademark.

The use in this publication of trade names, trademarks, service marks, and similar terms, even if they are not identified as such, is not to be taken as an expression of opinion as to whether or not they are subject to proprietary rights.

While the advice and information in this book are believed to be true and accurate at the date of publication, neither the authors nor the editors nor the publisher can accept any legal responsibility for any errors or omissions that may be made. The publisher makes no warranty, express or implied, with respect to the material contained herein.

Managing Director, Apress Media LLC: Welmoed Spahr
Acquisitions Editor: Shaul Elson
Development Editor: Laura Berendson
Coordinating Editor: Gryffin Winkler
Copy Editor: Kim Burton

Cover image by Lori Lo from Pixabay.com

Distributed to the book trade worldwide by Springer Science+Business Media New York, 1 New York Plaza, New York, NY 10004. Phone 1-800-SPRINGER, fax (201) 348-4505, e-mail orders-ny@springer-sbm.com, or visit www.springeronline.com. Apress Media, LLC is a Delaware LLC and the sole member (owner) is Springer Science + Business Media Finance Inc (SSBM Finance Inc). SSBM Finance Inc is a **Delaware** corporation.

For information on translations, please e-mail booktranslations@springernature.com; for reprint, paperback, or audio rights, please e-mail bookpermissions@springernature.com.

Apress titles may be purchased in bulk for academic, corporate, or promotional use. eBook versions and licenses are also available for most titles. For more information, reference our Print and eBook Bulk Sales web page at http://www.apress.com/bulk-sales.

Any source code or other supplementary material referenced by the author in this book is available to readers on GitHub (https://github.com/Apress). For more detailed information, please visit https://www.apress.com/gp/services/source-code.

If disposing of this product, please recycle the paper

*For all who embark on the journey of data
and technology —May you resist the pull of buzzwords,
choose fundamentals over fleeting trends, and craft
solutions that stand the test of time.*

Table of Contents

About the Authors xi

About the Technical Reviewer xiii

Acknowledgments xv

Introduction xvii

Chapter 1: Getting Started with Cloud Analytics 1

Time to Innovate 2

Key Cloud Computing Concepts 6

Meet Snowflake 12

Summary 15

Chapter 2: Getting Started with Snowflake 17

Introduction 17

Creating a Snowflake Account 18

    Snowflake Editions 19

    Cloud Providers and Regions 19

    Snowflake Pricing Model 20

    Creating an Account 21

Navigating Snowflake with Snowsight 21

Creating a Database and Warehouse in Snowflake 23

    Creating a Warehouse 23

    Create a Database 26

Loading Data into Snowflake 28

    Overview of Bulk Data Loading 28

    Bulk Data Loading Recommendations 30

Summary 35

TABLE OF CONTENTS

Chapter 3: Continuous Data Loading with Snowpipe and Dynamic Tables............ 37

Introduction to Data Loading Strategies for Snowflake 38

Loading Data Continuously 42

    Snowpipe Auto-Ingest 42

Snowpipe REST API Using AWS Lambda 53

Working with Dynamic Tables in Snowflake 54

    What Are Dynamic Tables? 54

    Why Use Dynamic Tables? 54

Summary 58

Chapter 4: Snowflake Administration and RBAC 59

Administering Roles and Users 60

    Enforcement Model 62

    Secondary Roles 64

    Working with Roles and Users (with RBAC) 65

    New Role Types: Database Roles and Application Roles 68

    Using Permifrost for RBAC in Snowflake 68

    Dynamic Data Masking 71

Administering Databases and Warehouses 73

    Managing Warehouses 73

    Managing Databases 74

    UNDROP DATABASE 75

    Zero-Copy Cloning 75

Administering Account Parameters 77

Administering Database Objects 78

Administering Data Shares 79

Administering Clustered Tables 80

Snowflake Materialized Views 81

Summary 83

TABLE OF CONTENTS

Chapter 5: Secure Data Sharing 85
    Benefits of Snowflake Data Sharing 86
    Understanding Share Objects 87
    Implementing Secure Table Sharing 89
    Data Sharing Using a Secure View 93
    Sharing Regular View vs. Materialized View 98
    Summary 99

Chapter 6: Getting Started with Snowpark 101
    Key Features of Snowpark 101
    Setting up Snowpark 103
    Snowpark DataFrame Operations 106
    User-Defined Functions 109
    Stored Procedures 110
    Machine Learning Integration with Snowpark 112
    Summary 115

Chapter 7: Snowflake with Apache Iceberg 117
    Data Platform Architecture 118
    Getting Started with Apache Iceberg 119
        The Role of a Catalog 120
    Summary 132

Chapter 8: Getting Started with Streamlit 133
    Streamlit Basics 134
        Key Features of Streamlit 134
    Integration with Snowflake 135
    Creating a Basic Streamlit App 136
    Creating Interactive Streamlit Apps 139
        Error Handling and Troubleshooting 142
    Summary 144

TABLE OF CONTENTS

Chapter 9: Designing a Modern Analytics Solution with Snowflake 145
Modern Analytics Solution Architecture 146
Snowflake Partner Ecosystem 148
    Building Analytics Solutions with Matillion ETL and Tableau 149
    Building Analytics Solution with Open Source Software 158
    Running a dbt Project 162
    Engineering Excellence with dbt Development 167
    Data Ingestion and Orchestration 169
    Summary 171

Chapter 10: Performance Optimization and Cost Monitoring 173
Understanding Snowflake Architecture for Optimization 174
Data Read Optimization 175
    Data Clustering and Partitioning 175
    Data Storage Best Practices 177
Data Processing Optimization 178
    Analyze Query Execution 178
    Optimization Techniques 178
    Leverage Caching 182
Warehouse Configuration Optimization 183
    Right-sizing Virtual Warehouses 183
    Scaling Policies 183
Administering Resource Consumption 184
    Virtual Warehouse Usage 184
    Data Storage Usage 185
    Data Transfer Usage 187

Chapter 11: Snowflake AI and ML 191

Overview and Key Features 191
Key Features 192
Data Discovery 200
Data Cleaning and Transformation 200
Best Practices for Using Snowflake ML 201
Summary 202

Chapter 12: Migrating to Snowflake 203

Data Warehouse Migration Scenarios 204
Startup or Small Business Analytics Scenario 204
On-Premise Analytics Scenario for Enterprises and Large Organizations 205
Cloud Analytics Modernization with Snowflake 207
Data Warehouse Migration Process 208
Organizational Part of the Migration Project 208
Technical Aspects of a Migration Project 215
Real-World Migration Project 216
Additional Resources 219
Summary 219

Index 221

About the Authors

Dmitry Anoshin is an experienced data leader and recognized expert in building and implementing business and digital intelligence solutions, with extensive experience across North America and Europe. Throughout his career, he has successfully delivered analytics, data engineering, and cloud transformation projects across various industries, including retail, finance, marketing, and e-commerce.

Currently, Dmitry leads large-scale data initiatives, overseeing the development of a petabyte-scale data platform designed to support machine learning experiments, data science models, business intelligence reporting, and secure data exchange—all while maintaining a strong focus on privacy compliance and security.

In addition to his professional work, Dmitry is the founder of Surfalytics, a community platform dedicated to helping aspiring data engineers and analysts gain practical experience, share knowledge, and build real-world skills. You can learn more at Surfalytics.com.

Dmitry Foshin is a lead data engineer with over 12 years of experience in IT and big data, specializing in delivering end-to-end data solutions that drive business insights. He has a strong track record of leading and implementing full-stack data analytics platforms, ranging from ingestion and transformation to data warehousing and reporting, leveraging Azure cloud services, Databricks, and modern business intelligence tools. Dmitry is a coauthor of multiple editions of the *Azure Data Factory Cookbook* (Packt Publishing) and has successfully delivered large-scale data engineering initiatives for leading fast-moving consumer goods (FMCG) corporations across Europe.

ABOUT THE AUTHORS

Donna Strok is a passionate data enthusiast. She currently leads Data Science and Engineering at IMDb, an Amazon company. With over a decade of experience transforming data into insights, she has worked with industry leaders, including Expedia Group, JPMorgan Chase, and Amazon. She holds a bachelor's degree in computer science and a master's degree in computer information systems.

Based in the picturesque Pacific Northwest, she calls Seattle home, where she lives with her spouse and her cat, Dwayne. When not diving into data, she's either planning her next international adventure or on a quest to discover hidden culinary gems and unique grocery stores around the world—believing that the best stories often start in the most unexpected places.

About the Technical Reviewer

Vijay Anand Karthikeyan is a seasoned data and analytics professional with nearly two decades of experience delivering secure, scalable, and fault-tolerant analytics platforms. Known for his customer-centric approach, Vijay has led impactful data transformations across multiple industries, enabling organizations to unlock the full potential of their data. He is also recognized for his thought leadership, technical blogs, and expert contributions to Snowflake events. With deep expertise in big data, cloud platforms, and advanced analytics, he leverages emerging AI/ML technologies to build intelligent data applications, empowering businesses to make data-driven decisions through innovative, high-performance solutions.

Acknowledgments

Thank you to my coauthors, Dmitry and Donna, for your collaboration and expertise. I'm grateful to my wife, Maria, for her support and to my son, Miron, for his smiles along the way. I would also like to thank my parents, Valery and Galina, and my brother, Ilia, for always believing in me. And finally, to the Snowflake communities: your shared knowledge continues to inspire.

—Dmitry Foshin

Introduction

Welcome to *Jumpstart Snowflake, 2nd Edition*—your practical guide to building and managing modern analytics solutions using one of the most powerful cloud data platforms available today.

Whether you're a data engineer, analyst, architect, or technical decision-maker, this book is designed to help you harness the full potential of Snowflake's cloud-native capabilities. As data ecosystems grow more complex, organizations demand scalable, secure, and high-performing platforms to deliver insights faster and more reliably. Snowflake was built to address this exact challenge.

This edition reflects Snowflake's rapid evolution and introduces new features that empower data professionals to build sophisticated analytics and data applications, including Snowpark, Apache Iceberg, and Streamlit. It also explores emerging use cases, such as integrating Snowflake with generative AI and cloud cost optimization—two areas of increasing relevance for modern data teams.

Who This Book Is For

This book is ideal for

- Data engineers and architects transitioning from legacy data warehouses
- Analytics professionals seeking to modernize their stack
- Teams adopting Snowflake for the first time or expanding its usage
- Anyone interested in building real-world data products and applications using Snowflake

Some experience with SQL, cloud platforms, or data warehousing will be helpful but not strictly required.

INTRODUCTION

How This Book Is Structured

The book is divided into 12 chapters, each designed to build on the last while remaining approachable as stand-alone topics.

- **Chapter 1** introduces the modern analytics landscape and how Snowflake fits into it.
- **Chapter 2** walks you through setting up and navigating Snowflake.
- **Chapter 3** covers data ingestion strategies using Snowpipe and Dynamic Tables.
- **Chapter 4** focuses on administration and security with RBAC.
- **Chapter 5** introduces secure data sharing within and across organizations.
- **Chapter 6** gets you started with Snowpark for writing complex applications.
- **Chapter 7** dives into Apache Iceberg for managing large-scale, versioned data.
- **Chapter 8** demonstrates how to build interactive data apps with Streamlit.
- **Chapter 9** shows how to design full-stack analytics solutions using Snowflake.
- **Chapter 10** covers best practices for performance tuning and cost monitoring.
- **Chapter 11** explores the intersection of Snowflake and generative AI.
- **Chapter 12** discusses strategies for migrating from legacy platforms to Snowflake.

We've taken a hands-on approach, using real-world examples and cases drawn from industry experience. You'll find practical guidance, tips, and patterns that you can apply directly to your own projects.

We hope this book helps you not just adopt Snowflake—but leverage it as a foundation for scalable, secure, and innovative data solutions.

Let's get started.

CHAPTER 1

Getting Started with Cloud Analytics

Don't shoot for the middle. Dare to think big. Disrupt. Revolutionize. Don't be afraid to form a sweeping dream that inspires, not only others, but yourself as well. Incremental innovation will not lead to real change—it only improves something slightly. Look for breakthrough innovations, change that will make a difference.

—Leonard Brody and David Raffa

Cloud technologies can change the way organizations do analytics. The cloud enables organizations to move quickly and utilize best-of-breed technologies. Traditionally, data warehouse and business intelligence (BI) projects were considered a serious investment and took years to build. They required a solid team of business intelligence, data warehouse, and data integration developers and architects. Moreover, they required significant investments, IT support, and hardware and resource purchases. Even if you had the team, budget, and hardware in place, there was still a chance you would fail.

The cloud computing concept isn't new, but it has only recently begun to be widely used for analytics use cases. The cloud creates access to near-infinite, low-cost storage, provides scalable computing, and gives you tools for building secure solutions. Finally, you pay only for what you use.

CHAPTER 1   GETTING STARTED WITH CLOUD ANALYTICS

This chapter covers the analytics market trends over the past decade and the evolution of data warehouses. It also covers key cloud concepts and introduces the Snowflake data warehouse and its unique architecture.

Time to Innovate

As data professionals, we have worked on many data warehouse projects. We have designed and implemented numerous enterprise data warehouse solutions across various industries. Some projects we built from scratch, and others we fixed. Moreover, we have migrated systems from "legacy" to modern massively parallel processing (MPP) platforms and leveraged extract-load-transform (ELT) to let the MPP data warehouse platform do the heavy lifting.

MPP is one of the core principles of analytics data warehousing, and it is still valid today. It is helpful to know about the alternative that existed before MPP was introduced, namely, symmetric multiprocessing. Figure 1-1 illustrates an easy example to help you understand the difference between symmetric multiprocessing (SMP) and MPP.

Figure 1-1. *SMP vs. MPP*

Let's look at a simple example. Imagine you have to do laundry. You have two options.

- Miss a party on Friday night, but visit the laundromat where you can run all your laundry loads in parallel because everyone else is at the party (This is MPP.)

- Visit the laundromat on Saturday and use just one washing machine (This is SMP.)

Running six washing machines at the same time should wash more clothes faster than running one at a time. It is this linear scalability of MPP systems that allows us to accomplish our tasks faster. Table 1-1 compares the SMP and MPP systems. If you work with a data warehouse, you are probably aware of these concepts. Snowflake innovates in this area and actually combines SMP and MPP.

Table 1-1. MPP vs. SMP

Model	Description
Massively parallel processing (MPP)	The coordinated processing of a single task by multiple processors, with each processor using its own operating system (OS) and memory and communicating with each other using some form of messaging interface. Usually, MPP is a share-nothing architecture.
Symmetric multiprocessing (SMP)	A tightly coupled multiprocessor system where processors share resources such as single instances of the OS, memory, I/O devices, and a common bus. SMP is a shared-disk architecture.

In our past work, Oracle was popular across enterprise organizations. All the data warehouse solutions had one thing in common: they were extremely expensive and required the purchase of hardware. For consulting companies, the hardware drove revenue; you could have an unprofitable consulting project, but a hardware deal would cover the yearly bonus.

Later, we saw the rise of Hadoop and big data. The Internet was full of news about the replacement of traditional data warehouses with Hadoop ecosystems. It was a good time for Java developers, who could enjoy coding and writing MapReduce jobs until the community released a bunch of SQL tools such as Hive, Presto, and so on. Instead of learning Java personally, we applied Pareto principles, where we could solve 20 percent of tasks using traditional data warehouse platforms and SQL to bring 80 percent of the value. (In reality, we think it was more like 80 percent of the cases produced 95 percent of the value.)

Later, we saw the rise of data science and machine learning, and developers started to learn R and Python. However, we found that we still needed ELT/ETL and a data warehouse in place; otherwise, these local R/Python scripts had no value. It was relatively easy to get a sample dataset and build a model using data mining techniques. However, it was a challenge to automate and scale this process because of a lack of computing power.

Then came data lakes. It was clear that a data warehouse couldn't fit all the data, and we couldn't store all the data in a data warehouse because it was expensive. If you aren't familiar with data lakes, see `https://medium.com/rock-your-data/getting-started-with-data-lake-4bb13643f9`.

Again, some parties argued that data lakes were new data warehouses, and everyone should immediately migrate their traditional solutions to data lakes using the Hadoop technology stack. We didn't believe that data lakes could replace the traditional SQL data warehouses based on our experience with BI and business users. However, a data lake can complement an existing data warehouse solution when there is a large volume of unstructured data, and we don't want to leverage the existing data warehouse because it lacks sufficient computing power and storage capabilities. Apache products such as Hive, Presto, and Impala helped us get SQL access for big data storage and leverage data lake data with traditional BI solutions. It is clear that this path is expensive, but it could work for large companies with sufficient resources and a strong IT team.

Data lakes offer a significant advantage over traditional data warehouses: a decoupling of compute and storage. Imagine a situation when you have a dedicated MPP cluster data warehouse, and you are out of storage or compute. You have to add one more node that has both storage and compute, and you have to pay for both, even if you are using only one of them. In data lake architecture, you could scale compute and storage independently. It offers numerous benefits, including the ability to scale analytics and achieve cost-effectiveness. However, this approach had disadvantages, such as the lack of ACID (atomicity, consistency, isolation, durability) capabilities that we had with traditional databases and data warehouse platforms. Table 1-2 covers ACID properties and gives an example.

Table 1-2. ACID Properties

Model	Description
Atomicity	Ensures that each transaction is treated as a single unit of work, which either completes fully or does not complete at all. If any part of the transaction fails, the entire transaction is rolled back, leaving the database in its previous state. For example, in a data warehouse, if you're updating multiple tables during a data load, atomicity ensures that either all updates are applied or none are to maintain data integrity.
Consistency	Ensures that any transaction brings the database from one valid state to another, maintaining the integrity of the data based on predefined rules and constraints. For example, if there are constraints like foreign keys or data types, consistency ensures that after the transaction, the data adheres to those rules.
Isolation	Guarantees that the execution of a transaction is independent of other transactions happening at the same time. This prevents conflicts between concurrent transactions. For example, in an analytics query, isolation ensures that even if multiple users are running queries or updating the data at the same time, they won't interfere with each other.
Durability	Ensures that once a transaction has been committed, it remains in the system, even in the case of a failure such as a power outage or system crash. For example, after loading data into a warehouse, durability guarantees that the data persists and is available even if the system restarts.

In 2013, we heard about data warehouses in the cloud, namely, Amazon Redshift. We didn't see a difference between the cloud edition of Amazon Redshift and the on-premise Teradata, but it was obvious that we could get the same results without buying an extremely expensive appliance. Even at that time, we noticed the one benefit of Redshift. It was built on top of the existing open source database Postgres. This meant we didn't really need to learn something new. We knew the MPP concept from Teradata, and we knew Postgres, so we could start to use Redshift immediately. It was a breath of fresh air in a world of big dinosaurs like Oracle and Teradata.

It should be obvious to you that Amazon Redshift wasn't a disruptive innovation. It was an incremental innovation that built on a foundation already in place. In other words, it was an improvement to the existing technology or system. That is the core difference between Snowflake and other cloud data warehouse platforms.

Amazon Redshift became quite popular, and other companies introduced their cloud data warehouse platforms. Nowadays, all big market vendors are building a data warehouse solution for the cloud.

As a result, Snowflake was a disruptive innovation. The founders of Snowflake collected all the pain points of the existing data warehouse platforms and came up with a new architecture and product that addresses modern data needs and allows organizations to move fast with limited budgets and small teams.

Everyone has their own journey. Some worked with big data technologies like Hadoop; others spent time with traditional data warehouse and BI solutions. But all of us have a common goal of helping our organizations to be truly data-driven. With the rise of cloud computing, we have many new opportunities to do our jobs better and faster. Moreover, cloud computing opened new ways of doing analytics. Snowflake was founded in 2012, came out in stealth mode in October 2014, and became generally available in June 2015. Snowflake brought innovation into the data warehouse world, and it is the new era of data warehousing.

Nowadays, we have three terms: data warehouse, data lake, and lake house. Databricks introduced the term *lake house* in 2020. The idea was to combine the best elements from data lakes and data warehouses in a single platform. It means a lake house could decouple storage and compute that could scale independently and more or less support ACID. There are three popular open source solutions in the market: Apache Iceberg, Apache Delta, and Apache Hudi. This book covers Apache Iceberg because Snowflake supports this open table format, and it is quite popular.

Later in the chapter, we discuss Snowflake architecture, and you can decide whether Snowflake is a data warehouse or a lake house.

Key Cloud Computing Concepts

Before jumping into Snowflake, let's cover key cloud fundamentals to help you better understand the value of the cloud platform.

Basically, cloud computing is a remote virtual pool of on-demand shared resources offering compute, storage, database, and network services that can be rapidly deployed at scale. Figure 1-2 shows the key elements of cloud computing.

CHAPTER 1 GETTING STARTED WITH CLOUD ANALYTICS

Figure 1-2. Key cloud computing terms

Table 1-3 defines the key terms of cloud computing. These are the building blocks for a cloud analytics solution as well as the Snowflake data warehouse.

Table 1-3. Key Terms for Cloud Computing

Term	Description
Compute	The "brain" to process our workload. It has the CPUs and RAM to run workloads and processes, in our case, data.
Databases	Traditional SQL or NoSQL databases that we can leverage for our applications and analytics solutions to store structured data.
Storage	Saves and stores data in raw format as files. It could be traditional text files, images, or audio. Any resource in the cloud that can store data is a storage resource.
Network	Provides resources for connectivity between other cloud services and consumers.
ML/AI	Provides special types of resources for heavy computations and analytics workloads.

It is important to mention hypervisors as a core element of cloud computing. Figure 1-3 shows a host with multiple virtual machines (VMs) and a hypervisor that is used to create a virtualized environment that allows multiple VMs to be deployed on a single physical host.

CHAPTER 1 GETTING STARTED WITH CLOUD ANALYTICS

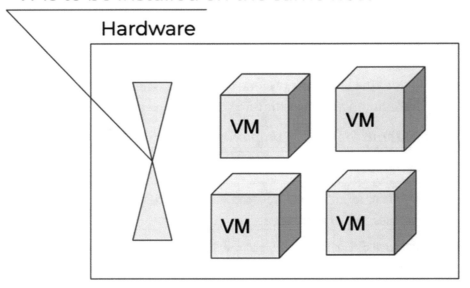

Figure 1-3. *Hypervisor role*

Virtualization offers the following benefits.

- Reduces capital expenditure
- Reduces operating costs
- Provides a smaller footprint
- Provides optimization for resources

There are three cloud deployment models, as shown in Figure 1-4.

Figure 1-4. Cloud deployment models

The model you choose depends on the organization's data handling policies and security requirements. For example, often government and health organizations that have a lot of critical customer information prefer to keep the data in a private cloud. Table 1-4 defines the cloud deployment models.

Table 1-4. Cloud Deployment Models

Model	Description
Public cloud	The service provider opens the cloud infrastructure for organizations to use, and the infrastructure is on the premises of the service provider (data centers), but it is operated by the organization paying for it.
Private cloud	The cloud is solely owned by a particular institution, organization, or enterprise.
Hybrid cloud	This is a mix of public and private clouds.

In most cases, we prefer to go with a public cloud. Amazon Web Services (AWS), Microsoft Azure, and Google Cloud Platform are all public clouds, and you can start building solutions and applications immediately.

It is also good to know about cloud service models (as opposed to on-premise solutions). Figure 1-5 shows the three main service models with an easy analogy: "Hamburger as a Service."

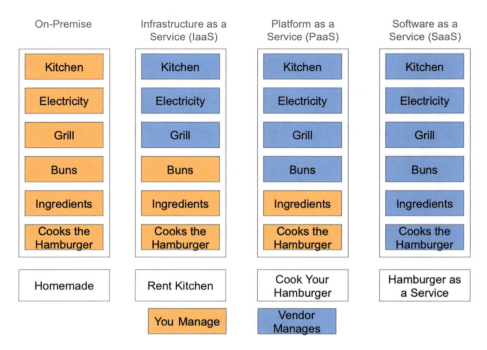

Figure 1-5. *Cloud service models*

One example of IaaS is a cloud virtual machine. Amazon EC2 is an example of IaaS. Amazon Elastic MapReduce (i.e., managed Hadoop) and Amazon Redshift are examples of PaaS, and DynamoDB (AWS NoSQL database) and Lambda are examples of SaaS, which is completely managed for you.

Note In a cloud software distribution model, SaaS is the most comprehensive service, and it abstracts much of the underlying hardware and software maintenance from the end user. It is characterized by a seamless, web-based experience, with as little management and optimization as possible required of the end user. The IaaS and PaaS models, comparatively, often require significantly more management of the underlying hardware or software.

Snowflake is a SaaS model also known as a *data warehouse as a service* (DWaaS). Everything—from the database storage infrastructure to the compute resources used for analysis and the optimization of data within the database—is handled by Snowflake. What does it mean for a data engineer? Let's review an example with Amazon Redshift.

Imagine that you are building a data warehouse, and you have to create a fact table with billions of rows. You have to decide on the data distribution style for this fact table. Amazon Redshift is MPP, and it has multiple nodes. Our goal is to equally distribute the data. The performance of the data warehouse will depend on these decisions, and in case of wrong design, it would be painful and time-consuming to make the change. By the way, this was the typical data engineering work. In the case of Snowflake, this process is managed by Snowflake. We could ingest terabytes of data into the fact table, and Snowflake would manage the data distribution and make sure it is stored in the most efficient way. You learn more about this in the book.

It is worth mentioning that despite the fact that Snowflake had a great start with its unique product offering, DWaaS, its close competitors are also heavily investing in innovations to match the offering for their customers. We already mentioned Amazon Redshift as the first true cloud MPP data warehouse. Redshift released new instance types RA3 at the end of 2019 to address their limitations of scaling compute and storage independently. AWS released Amazon Redshift Serverless in 2022, which allows you to manage workloads without setting up clusters.

A final aspect of cloud computing theory is the shared responsibility model (SRM). Figure 1-6 shows the key elements of SRM.

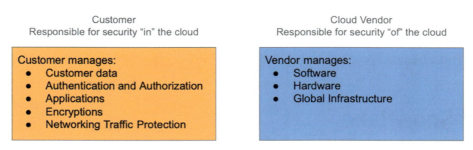

Figure 1-6. *Cloud vendors shared responsibility model*

SRM has many attributes, but the main idea is that the cloud vendor is responsible for the security *of* the cloud, and the customers are responsible for the security *in* the cloud. This means that the clients should define their security strategies and leverage best practices for their data to keep it secure.

When we talk about the cloud, you should know that cloud resources are hosted in data centers, and there is a concept of a region. You can find information about Snowflake availability for the different cloud vendors and regions at `https://docs.snowflake.net/manuals/user-guide/intro-regions.html`.

CHAPTER 1   GETTING STARTED WITH CLOUD ANALYTICS

Before moving to the next section, refer to Figure 1-7, which shows how long data takes to upload to the cloud; this reference comes from the Google Cloud Platform presentation.

Bandwidth	1 GB	10 GB	100 GB	1 TB	10 TB	100 TB	1 PB	10 PB	100 PB
1 Mbps	3 hours	30 hours	12 days	124 days	3 years	34 years	340 years	3404 years	34048 years
10 Mbps	18 minutes	3 hours	30 hours	12 days	124 days	3 years	34 years	340 years	3404 years
100 Mbps	2 minutes	18 minutes	3 hours	30 hours	12 days	124 days	3 years	34 years	340 years
1 Gbps	11 seconds	2 minutes	18 minutes	3 hours	30 hours	12 days	124 days	3 years	34 years
10 Gbps	1 second	11 seconds	2 minutes	18 minutes	3 hours	30 hours	12 days	124 days	3 years
100 Gbps	0.1 seconds	1 second	11 seconds	2 minutes	18 minutes	3 hours	30 hours	12 days	124 days

Figure 1-7. Modern bandwidth

This table is a useful reference when migrating a data warehouse from an on-premise solution to the cloud. You learn more about data warehouse migration and modernization in Chapter 14.

Meet Snowflake

Snowflake is the first data warehouse that was built for the cloud from the ground up, and it is a first-in-class DWaaS. Snowflake runs on the most popular cloud providers, such as Amazon Web Services and Microsoft Azure. Moreover, Snowflake has announced availability on Google Cloud Platform. As a result, we can deploy the data warehouse platform on any of the major cloud vendors. Snowflake is faster and easier to use and far more flexible than a traditional data warehouse. It handles all aspects of authentication, configurations, resource management, data protection, availability, and optimization.

CHAPTER 1 GETTING STARTED WITH CLOUD ANALYTICS

It is easy to get started with Snowflake. You just need to choose the right edition of Snowflake and sign up. You can start with a free trial and learn about the key features of Snowflake or compare it with other data warehouse platforms at https://trial.snowflake.com. You can immediately load your data and get insights. All the components of Snowflake services run in a public cloud infrastructure.

Note Snowflake cannot be run on private cloud infrastructures (on-premises or hosted). It is not a packaged software offering that can be installed by a user. Snowflake manages all aspects of software installation and updates.

Snowflake was built from the ground up and designed to handle modern big data and analytics challenges. It combines the benefits of both SMP and MPP architectures and takes full advantage of the cloud. Figure 1-8 shows the architecture of Snowflake.

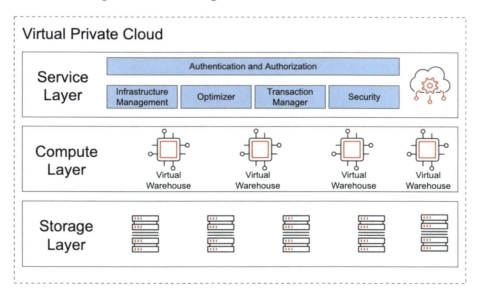

Figure 1-8. *Snowflake architecture*

Similar to an SMP architecture, Snowflake uses a central storage that is accessible from all the compute nodes. In addition, similar to an MPP architecture, Snowflake processes queries using MPP compute clusters, also known as *virtual warehouses*. As a result, Snowflake combines the simplicity of data management and scalability with a shared-nothing architecture (like in MPP).

CHAPTER 1 GETTING STARTED WITH CLOUD ANALYTICS

As shown in Figure 1-8, the Snowflake architecture consists of three main layers. Table 1-5 describes each layer.

Table 1-5. Key Layers of Snowflake

Layer	Description
Service layer	It consists of services that coordinate Snowflake's work. Services run on a dedicated instance and include authentication, infrastructure management, metadata management, query parsing and optimization, and access control.
Compute layer	It consists of virtual warehouses, and each is an MPP compute cluster comprising multiple compute nodes. Each VW is an independent compute cluster that doesn't share resources with other VWs.
Storage layer	It stores data in an internal compressed columnar format using cloud storage. For example, in AWS, it is S3; in Azure, it is Blob storage. Snowflake manages all aspects of data storage, and customers don't have direct access to file storage. Data is accessible only via SQL.

In other words, Snowflake offers almost unlimited computing and storage capabilities by utilizing cloud storage and computing. Let's look at a simple example of a traditional organization with a data warehouse platform. For example, say you have a data warehouse, and you run ETL (extract-transform-load) processing overnight. During heavy ETL processing, business users can't use the data warehouse a lot, and there aren't many resources available.

At the same time, the marketing department should run complex queries to calculate the attribution model. The inventory team should run their reports and optimize inventory. In other words, every process and every team in the organization is important, but the data warehouse is a bottleneck. In the case of Snowflake, every team or department can have its own virtual warehouse that can be scaled up and down immediately, depending on the requirements. Moreover, the ETL process can have its own virtual warehouse that is running only overnight. This means the data warehouse isn't a bottleneck anymore and allows the organization to unlock its data's potential. Moreover, the organization pays only for the resources it uses. You don't have to buy expensive appliances or think about future workloads. Snowflake is truly democratizing data and gives almost unlimited power to business users.

In addition to scalability and simplicity, Snowflake offers many more unique features that didn't exist before and aren't available in other data warehouse platforms (cloud or on-premise), such as data sharing, time travel, database replication and failover, zero-copy cloning, and more that is discussed in this book.

Summary

This chapter briefly reviewed the history of data warehousing and covered the fundamentals of cloud computing. This information provides some background, allowing you to gain a better understanding of why Snowflake was introduced to the market and why the cloud is the future of data warehousing and modern analytics. You also learned about the unique architecture of Snowflake and its key layers. In the next chapter, you learn how to start working with Snowflake.

CHAPTER 2

Getting Started with Snowflake

Congratulations on choosing to get started with Snowflake! This chapter guides you through the essentials of this powerful cloud data platform. It covers planning your Snowflake environment, creating a Snowflake account, and navigating the web-based user interface. You learn how to create a database and a virtual warehouse in Snowflake. The chapter also introduces data loading techniques, including using the VARIANT data type and fundamental SQL queries. By the end of this chapter, you will be ready to embark on your cloud analytics journey and explore the more advanced capabilities of Snowflake covered in later chapters.

Introduction

In today's data-driven world, organizations need robust and scalable solutions to effectively manage and analyze their data. Snowflake has emerged as a leading cloud data platform, offering a unique architecture that separates storage and compute, enabling businesses to scale their data warehousing needs seamlessly. This chapter provides a comprehensive guide to help you get started with Snowflake and covers the following topics.

- **Creating a Snowflake account**: We walk you through the process of setting up your free trial Snowflake account, guiding you through the choices of Snowflake editions, cloud providers, and regions.

- **Navigating the Snowflake user interface**: Become familiar with the intuitive web-based interface of Snowflake. We explore its key components, including Worksheets for running queries, Databases for storing data, and Warehouses for providing compute power.

- **Creating a database and warehouse**: Learn how to create your first database to store your data and a virtual warehouse to process your queries. We provide clear SQL examples to help you get started quickly.

- **Loading data into Snowflake**: Discover how to load data from various sources into Snowflake. We cover supported file formats, the use of stages as temporary storage areas, and the essential PUT and COPY INTO commands. Additionally, you learn how to leverage the versatile VARIANT data type to handle semi-structured data like JSON.

Let's get started!

Creating a Snowflake Account

It's crucial to plan your Snowflake environment carefully. This section guides you through the essential considerations and steps to set up your Snowflake account. As a prerequisite, we touch on the following before creating your Snowflake account.

- Snowflake editions
- Cloud providers and regions
- Snowflake pricing model
- Types of Snowflake tools

CHAPTER 2 GETTING STARTED WITH SNOWFLAKE

Snowflake Editions

Snowflake offers different editions to cater to various needs and budgets. Table 2-1 is a concise overview of the Snowflake editions. Be sure to check Snowflake's website for the latest offerings.

Table 2-1. *Snowflake Editions*

Edition	Key Features and Considerations
Standard	Ideal for small to medium-sized businesses with moderate data needs
Enterprise	Designed for larger organizations with demanding performance requirements
Business Critical	Offers enhanced security and compliance features for sensitive data
Virtual Private Snowflake (VPS)	Provides a dedicated Snowflake environment for maximum isolation and control

Cloud Providers and Regions

Snowflake is available on major cloud providers, including Amazon Web Services (AWS), Microsoft Azure, and Google Cloud Platform (GCP). Each cloud provider has data centers in many locations around the world. These locations are referred to as *regions*. Transferring data between regions can have cost implications. Therefore, region considerations are important because the costs can vary depending on your requirements.

Multiple regions may be necessary to address global data access speeds and replication needs. For example, if you have users located in different parts of the world, it might make sense to replicate or partition the data closer to your users. If you have a use case for multiple regions, then you need to create a Snowflake account for each region.

Note Snowflake accounts do not support more than one region. You must create a Snowflake account for each region.

Regions dictate only the geographic location of where the data is stored and the compute resources are provisioned, not the usage of the data. The data can be used from anywhere in the world. Also, the cloud platform that is chosen for each Snowflake account is completely independent of your other Snowflake accounts. You may choose to use a mix of cloud providers and regions; however, be aware that this impacts the cost of transferring data into your Snowflake account. Also, there might be limitations with the cloud provider or region you are considering. Please visit Snowflake's website (`https://docs.snowflake.com/en/user-guide/intro-regions`) for the most update-to-date information.

Snowflake Pricing Model

Snowflake's pricing model is based on a consumption-based system of credits, meaning you pay only for the resources you actually use. Let's explore how these credits relate to the core components: storage, compute, and data transfer.

> **Storage**: Snowflake's charge for data storage considers data compression. This means that you only pay for the compressed size of your data, which can lead to significant cost savings compared to other data warehousing solutions that charge for uncompressed data.
>
> **Compute**: The compute costs are determined by the size of the virtual warehouse you choose for processing queries and loading data. Virtual warehouses are essentially clusters of compute resources that can be scaled up or down as needed. Larger warehouses offer more compute power but also consume credits at a faster rate. Snowflake offers eight different virtual warehouse sizes, each with a different credit consumption rate. For example, assume you choose a "large" virtual warehouse for a particular task. This warehouse size corresponds to 8 credits per hour. If the task runs for 30 minutes (0.5 hours), you are billed for 4 credits (8 credits per hour * 0.5 hours).
>
> **Data transfer**: While Snowflake doesn't charge for loading data from external stages like Amazon S3 or Microsoft Azure into your Snowflake environment, you may incur egress fees from your

cloud storage provider if your data is stored in a different region or network than your Snowflake account. Additionally, there are charges for exporting data out of Snowflake to an external storage location, which include the compute costs for the export query and potential egress charges if the target location differs by region or cloud provider.

Creating an Account

Snowflake offers a 30-day free trial with a set amount of credits to explore its features. To begin, navigate to `www.snowflake.com` and click **Start for Free**. You are prompted to provide information like your name, company name, email address, phone number, desired Snowflake edition, cloud provider, and region. After submitting the form, you receive an email with a link to activate your account. It's essential to activate your account within 72 hours to avoid having to create a new trial account.

During your account creation, you received an email that notified you that your account has been provisioned. This email contains a link to your Snowflake web interface and a link to activate your account. Clicking **Activate** takes you to a web browser screen where you are prompted to create a username and password. Once you have entered your desired username and password, the "Welcome to Snowflake" web interface will appear. Congratulations, you have officially logged into Snowflake!

Once you've successfully activated your Snowflake account, you can access the Snowflake web interface, which is explored in the next section.

Navigating Snowflake with Snowsight

Now that you've created your Snowflake account, you can set up your environment through the Snowflake user interface (UI). There are two that your account may have access to: Classic Console and Snowsight. Both UIs perform the same functions. Snowflake is currently upgrading all accounts to Snowsight through stages. Eventually, all accounts will only have access to Snowsight; thus, this section focuses on Snowsight.

Snowsight is like a visual control panel for managing your data warehousing environment. Snowsight is made up of four key sections: the navigation menu, search, quick actions, and recently viewed (see Figure 2-1).

CHAPTER 2   GETTING STARTED WITH SNOWFLAKE

- **Navigation** is the central hub for accessing and managing various components within Snowsight. You can use it to create and manage your data products, notebooks, worksheets, databases, and other related artifacts.

- **Search bar** enables you to quickly locate specific content within your Snowflake environment. You can search for navigation menu items and database objects like tables, columns, functions, and more.

- **Quick actions** provides shortcuts to frequently used operations tailored to your current role. Examples of quick actions include querying data using a sheet, uploading file directions to tables, and worksheets for use with Python code.

- **Recently viewed** keeps track of activity, which helps navigate. You may also create different content types.

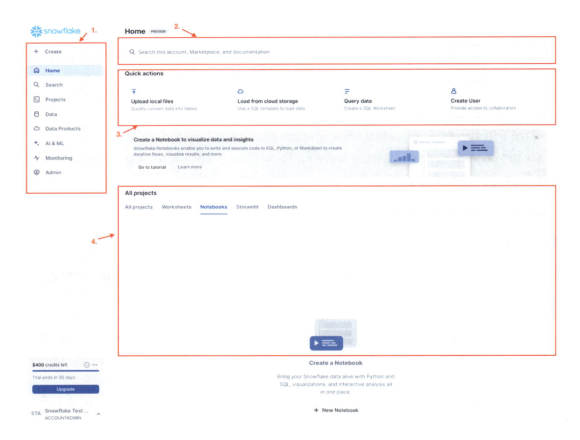

Figure 2-1. *Reviewing Snowsight UI*

CHAPTER 2   GETTING STARTED WITH SNOWFLAKE

Creating a Database and Warehouse in Snowflake

Databases and warehouses are fundamental components of Snowflake's architecture, playing crucial roles in data storage and processing. Understanding these concepts is essential for efficient platform usage. A **database** acts as a *logical container* for storing related datasets in a structured manner. This logical separation helps organize data and manage access control. For instance, different departments within an organization or different applications might have separate databases. A **warehouse** provides the *compute power* necessary for querying and processing data stored in databases. Warehouses operate independently of databases, allowing flexible scaling based on specific needs. Let's start with creating a warehouse first.

Creating a Warehouse

Let's review the two ways to create a warehouse: through the Snowflake web interface and using a SQL command.

CREATE WAREHOUSE: WEB INTERFACE

1. Log in to your Snowflake web interface.
2. Click **Admin + Warehouses**.
3. Click **+ Warehouse** (upper right corner).
4. Give your warehouse a name and description. Figure 2-2 shows the information entered into the web interface.
    a. Choose a **Type** and **Size**. For this exercise, we left the defaults.
    b. Make modifications to **Advanced Options**. For this exercise, we left the defaults.

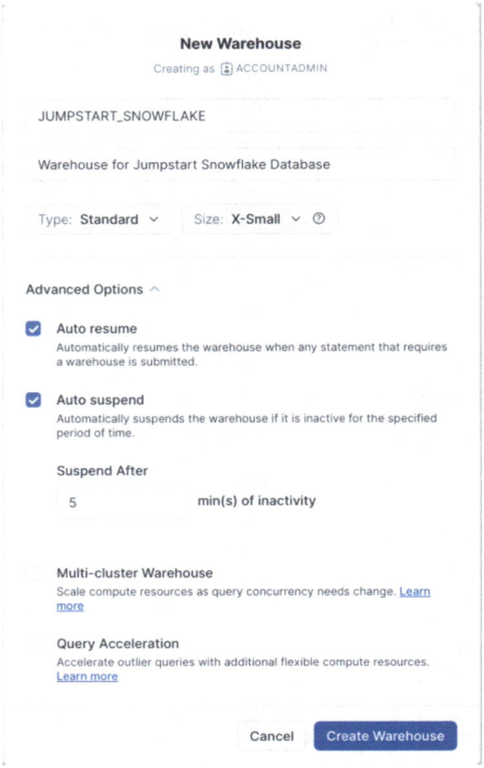

CHAPTER 2   GETTING STARTED WITH SNOWFLAKE

Figure 2-2. Creating a new warehouse through the web interface

---

CREATE WAREHOUSE: SQL COMMAND

This example executes the SQL command through a Snowflake worksheet through the Snowflake UI, though you can use a SQL client that is already connected to your Snowflake account.

1. Click **Worksheets**.

2. Click **+ (Create SQL Worksheet)** in the upper right corner.

3. Execute the following CREATE WAREHOUSE command.

    ```
    CREATE WAREHOUSE JUMPSTART_SNOWFLAKE_SQL
    WITH WAREHOUSE_TYPE = 'STANDARD'
    WAREHOUSE_SIZE = 'XSMALL'
    ```

CHAPTER 2 GETTING STARTED WITH SNOWFLAKE

```
    AUTO_SUSPEND = 600
    AUTO_RESUME = TRUE;
```

4. Figure 2-3 shows that our warehouse, **JUMPSTART_SNOWFLAKE_SQL**, has been successfully created.

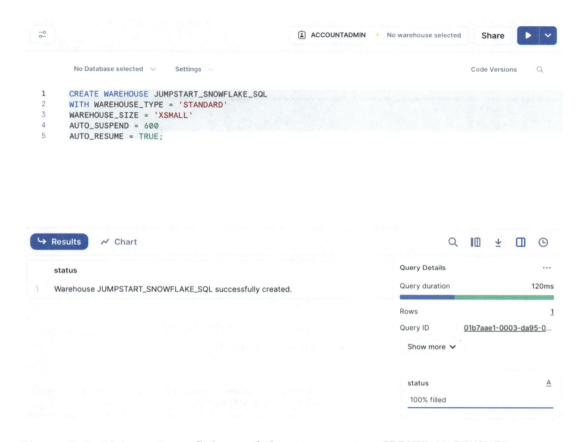

Figure 2-3. *Using a Snowflake worksheet to execute a CREATE WAREHOUSE statement shows that the warehouse was successfully created*

Caution   Always ensure that auto suspend and auto resume are set in your warehouse. By default, these settings are set for you when a virtual warehouse is provisioned. Auto suspend stops a warehouse if it sits idle for a specified period of time, while auto resume starts a suspended virtual warehouse when queries are submitted to it. This is important because a running warehouse will consume Snowflake credits only when compute resources are being utilized. Shutting down your warehouse when it is not in use helps conserve energy and control costs.

Create a Database

Now that you have created a warehouse, let's create a database! Similar to a warehouse, you can also create a database through the Snowflake web interface or a SQL command. While creating a database, users can specify several key parameters.

- **Database name**: Serves as a unique identifier for the database within the Snowflake account.
- **Database owner**: Has full privileges on the database.
- **Other relevant properties**: Parameters related to security, replication, and more, depending on the specific needs.

CREATE DATABASE: WEB INTERFACE

1. Click **Data + Databases**.
2. Click **+Database** (upper right corner).
3. Give your database a **Name** and **Comment** (description) (see Figure 2-4).

CHAPTER 2   GETTING STARTED WITH SNOWFLAKE

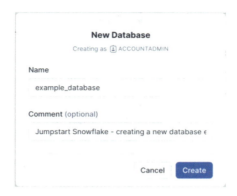

Figure 2-4. *Creating a new database through web interface*

4. Click **Create**.

5. After the database is created, you may edit permissions, add schemas, clone, drop, or transfer ownership by clicking the ellipses (see Figure 2-5).

Figure 2-5. *Clicking the ellipses gives options for your selected database*

CREATE DATABASE: SQL COMMAND

To create the same database using a SQL command, execute the following statement in a SQL client that is connected to your Snowflake database. You can execute SQL commands in Snowflake worksheets within the Snowsight web interface.

```
create DATABASE IDENTIFIER('"EXAMPLE_DATABASE"') COMMENT = 'Jumpstart
Snowflake - creating a new database example'
```

CHAPTER 2   GETTING STARTED WITH SNOWFLAKE

Loading Data into Snowflake

Now that you have set up your database and warehouse in Snowflake, you need to load your data. Snowflake is designed to efficiently handle this process and supports diverse data loading methods, sources, and formats. For smaller datasets or initial testing, you can load data directly from local files into Snowflake. However, as your data needs grow, using Snowflake's integration with cloud storage services like Amazon S3, Azure Blob Storage, and Google Cloud Storage becomes more advantageous. Directly loading data from these platforms is especially beneficial for handling large datasets, enabling you to create robust and efficient data pipelines. This approach streamlines the data ingestion process and allows you to seamlessly integrate your data workflows with existing cloud storage solutions.

There are two ways to load data into Snowflake: bulk data loading with the COPY statement and continuous data loading with Snowpipe. This chapter is focused on bulk data loading. It covers the following topics.

- **Overview of bulk data loading**: We explain what bulk data loading is, file load locations, supported file formats and encoding, compression handling, and encryption options.

- **Bulk data loading recommendations**: We discuss file preparation, including file sizing and splitting, the CSV and semi-structured formats, staging, loading, and querying.

Note   Continuous data loading with Snowpipe is covered in Chapter 3.

Overview of Bulk Data Loading

The bulk loading of data using COPY has been done longer than Snowflake has been around. Many other database management systems support using the COPY statement. Therefore, it is no surprise that Snowflake offers the same support. To better understand bulk data loading, let's review and answer some key questions.

- What is bulk data loading?

- Where can we bulk data load from?

CHAPTER 2   GETTING STARTED WITH SNOWFLAKE

- What are the compression and encryption options?
- What file formats are supported?

To get data into a database table, you need to insert it. Insert statements can take a while since they need to be executed one row at a time. Bulk copying can take a large amount of data and insert it into a database all in one batch. The bulk data loading option in Snowflake allows batch loading of data from files that are in cloud storage, like AWS S3.

If your data files are not currently in cloud storage, then there is an option to copy the data files from a local machine to a cloud storage *staging area* before loading them into Snowflake. This is known as Snowflake's *internal* staging area. The data files are transmitted from a local machine to an internal, Snowflake-designated, cloud storage staging location and then loaded into tables using the COPY command.

Snowflake supports loading data from files staged in any of the following cloud storage locations, regardless of the cloud platform for your Snowflake account.

- Snowflake-designated internal storage staging location
- AWS S3, where files can be loaded directly from any user-supplied S3 bucket
- GCP Cloud Storage, where files can be loaded directly from any user-supplied GCP cloud storage container
- Azure Blob storage, where files can be loaded directly from any user-supplied Azure container

---

Note   Data transfer billing charges may apply when loading data from files staged across different platforms.

Compression Handling

When staging uncompressed files in a Snowflake stage, the files are automatically compressed using gzip, unless compression is explicitly disabled. Snowflake can automatically detect gzip, bzip2, deflate, and raw_deflate compression methods. Autodetection is not yet supported for brotli and zstandard. Therefore, when staging or loading files compressed with either of these methods, you must explicitly specify the compression method that was used.

Encryption Options

When staging unencrypted files in an internal Snowflake location, the files are automatically encrypted using 128-bit keys. 256-bit keys can be enabled (for stronger encryption); however, additional configuration is required. Files that are already encrypted can be loaded into Snowflake from external cloud storage; the key used to encrypt the files must be provided to Snowflake.

Supported File Formats and Encoding

Snowflake supports most of the common file formats used for loading data. These file formats include the following.

- Delimited files (any valid delimiter is supported; the default is a comma)
- JSON and XML
- Avro, including the automatic detection and processing of staged Avro files that were compressed using Snappy
- ORC, including the automatic detection and processing of staged ORC files that were compressed using Snappy or zlib
- Parquet, including the automatic detection and processing of staged Parquet files that were compressed using Snappy

For delimited files, the default character set is UTF-8. To use any other characters set, you must explicitly specify the encoding to use for loading. For all other supported file formats (JSON, Avro, etc.), the only supported character set is UTF-8.

Bulk Data Loading Recommendations

Loading large datasets can affect query performance. Snowflake recommends dedicating separate warehouses to loading and querying operations to optimize the performance of each. This section covers the recommended ways to prepare the files.

File Preparation and Sizing

The number of data files that can be processed in parallel is determined by the number and capacity of servers in a warehouse. If you follow the file sizing guidelines described in the following section, the data loading requires minimal resources. Note that these recommendations apply to both bulk data loads and continuous loading using Snowpipe. Here's what to know about file sizing.

- The number of load operations that can run in parallel cannot exceed the number of data files to be loaded.

- To optimize the number of parallel operations for a load, Snowflake recommends producing data files roughly 100 MB to 250 MB in size, compressed.

- Aggregate smaller files to minimize the processing overhead for each file.

- Split larger files into a greater number of smaller files to distribute the load among the servers in an active warehouse. The number of data files processed in parallel is determined by the number and capacity of servers in a warehouse.

- Snowflake recommends splitting large files by line to avoid records that span chunks.

- Data loads of large Parquet files (e.g., greater than 3 GB) could time out. Split large files into files 1 GB in size (or smaller) for loading.

If your source database does not allow you to export data files in smaller chunks, use a third-party utility to split large CSV files. Windows does not include a native file split utility; however, Windows supports many third-party tools and scripts that can split large data files. Linux has the `split` utility, which enables you to split a CSV file into multiple smaller files.

> **Note** Splitting larger data files allows the load to scale linearly. Using a larger warehouse (X-Large, 2X-Large, etc.) consumes more credits and may not result in any performance increase.

CSV File Preparation

Consider the following guidelines when preparing your delimited text (CSV) files for loading.

- UTF-8 is the default character set; however, additional encodings are supported. Use the ENCODING file format option to specify the character set for the data files.

- Snowflake supports ASCII characters (including high-order characters) as delimiters. Common field delimiters include the pipe (|), comma (,), caret (^), and tilde (~).

- A field can be optionally enclosed by double quotes, and, within the field, all special characters are automatically escaped, except the double quote itself needs to be escaped by having two double quotes right next to each other (""). For unenclosed fields, a backslash (\) is the default escape character.

- Common escape sequences can be used (e.g., \t for tab, \n for newline, \r for carriage return, and \\ for backslash).

- Fields containing carriage returns should also be enclosed in quotes (single or double).

- The number of columns in each row should be consistent.

Semi-Structured Data File Preparation and VARIANT values

Semi-structured data is data that does not conform to the standards of traditional structured data, but it contains tags or other types of markup that identify individual, distinct entities within the data.

Two of the key attributes that distinguish semi-structured data from structured data are nested data structures and the lack of a fixed schema.

- Structured data requires a fixed schema that is defined before the data can be loaded and queried in a relational database system. Semi-structured data does not require a prior definition of a schema and can constantly evolve; i.e., new attributes can be added at any time.

- In addition, entities within the same class may have different attributes even though they are grouped together, and the order of the attributes is not important.

- Unlike structured data, which represents data as a flat table, semi-structured data can contain *n* level of hierarchies of nested information.

The steps for loading semi-structured data into tables are identical to those for loading structured data into relational tables. Snowflake loads semi-structured data into a single VARIANT column. You can also use a COPY INTO table statement during data transformation to extract selected columns from a staged data file into separate table columns.

When semi-structured data is inserted into a VARIANT column, what Snowflake is really doing is extracting information about the key locations and values and saving it into a semi-structured document. The document is referenced by the metadata engine for fast SQL retrieval.

Note VARIANT "null" values (not to be confused with SQL NULL values) are not loaded to the table. To avoid this, extract semi-structured data elements containing "null" values into relational columns before loading them. Alternatively, if the "null" values in your files indicate missing values and have no other special meaning, Snowflake recommends setting the file format option STRIP_NULL_VALUES to TRUE when loading the semi-structured data files.

File Staging

Both internal and external stage locations in Snowflake can include a path (referred to as a *prefix* in AWS). When staging regular datasets, Snowflake recommends partitioning the data into logical paths to identify details such as geographical location, along with the date when the data is written.

Organizing your data files by path allows you to copy the data into Snowflake with a single command. This allows you to execute concurrent COPY statements that match a subset of files, taking advantage of parallel operations.

CHAPTER 2 GETTING STARTED WITH SNOWFLAKE

For example, if you were storing data for a company that did business all over the world, you might include identifiers such as continent, country, and city in paths along with data write dates (e.g., NA/Mexico/Quintana_Roo/Cancun/2024/01/01/01/).

When planning regular data loads, such as with extract-transform-load (ETL) processing, it is important to partition the data in your internal (i.e., Snowflake) stage or external locations (S3 buckets or Azure containers) using logical, granular paths. Create a partitioning structure that includes identifying details such as the application or location, along with the date when the data was written. You can then copy any fraction of the partitioned data into Snowflake with a single command. You can copy data into Snowflake by the hour, day, month, or even year when you initially populate tables.

Here are some examples of partitioned S3 buckets using paths.

- s3://bucket_name/brand/2024/07/01/11/
- s3://bucket_name/region/country/2024/07/01/14/

Loading

The COPY command supports several options for loading data files from a stage.

- By path of internal location or prefix of external location
- By listing specific files to load (up to 1000 per COPY command)
- By using pattern matching to identify specific files by pattern

These options enable you to copy a fraction of the staged data into a Snowflake table with a single command. This allows you to execute concurrent COPY statements that match a subset of files, taking advantage of parallel operations. Do take special note that the file being copied must have the same data structure (i.e., number of columns, data type) as the table.

Tip   Listing specific files to load from a stage is generally the fastest option.

Exercises

Snowflake has tutorials for bulk loading data from the local file system and S3. For more information, please see Snowflake's tutorials.

- **Local file systems**: `https://docs.snowflake.com/en/user-guide/tutorials/data-load-internal-tutorial`
- **External data (S3)**: `https://docs.snowflake.com/en/user-guide/tutorials/data-load-external-tutorial`

Summary

This chapter has guided you through the essentials of getting started with Snowflake, the powerful cloud data platform. You've explored the different editions of Snowflake and learned how to create your free trial account. You should now be familiar with the various cloud providers and regions available, as well as the key considerations for selecting the best combination for your needs. Understanding Snowflake's consumption-based pricing model, which charges you based on storage, compute, and data transfer, is crucial for managing costs.

You also learned how to create a database and a virtual warehouse, providing the foundation for your data warehousing activities. And you were introduced to data loading techniques in Snowflake, which is a fundamental aspect of any data warehousing solution. The knowledge and skills gained from this chapter empower you to explore the more advanced capabilities of Snowflake covered in later chapters.

CHAPTER 3

Continuous Data Loading with Snowpipe and Dynamic Tables

You and I are streaming data engines.

— Jeff Hawkins

If you're a data analyst or data scientist or you're on an executive team, you know the value of access to continuous and timely data at any given time. You want to know that whenever you're querying data, transforming it, or accessing it in any way, the data represents the most up-to-date information available to use for data analysis.

If you have stale data, you might make inaccurate conclusions or have skewed statistics that will lead to misinformed strategic decisions that can affect your company down the line. Access to continuous data is a beneficial thing for anyone, regardless of role.

Nowadays, we know that data is generated much faster than it ever used to be before. In the past, corporate data would be updated infrequently, either daily, weekly, or even monthly, and added to your data warehouse. Data accumulates over time, which leads to it becoming more and more challenging to process.

Now, we have app data, mobile data, and data sensors that generate this constant flow of useful analytical data, but it can really be a challenge to get it into a data warehouse because it's being generated so quickly. Multitudes of tiny files are being generated, and that can definitely lead to problems.

This chapter begins with an overview of data loading strategies in Snowflake, highlighting their advantages and trade-offs. Next, we introduce Snowpipe, a serverless ingestion service that allows automated data loading as new files arrive in cloud storage. You'll learn how to set up Snowpipe auto-ingest for event-driven loading and use the Snowpipe REST API for custom integrations. Finally, we explore dynamic tables, which enable continuous transformation of streaming and batch data within Snowflake. Hands-on exercises reinforce these concepts, guiding you through building pipelines using both Snowpipe and dynamic tables.

This chapter builds on earlier discussions of Snowflake's architecture and ingestion methods, providing essential knowledge for those looking to implement near real-time data pipelines. Whether you are designing streaming analytics, real-time dashboards, or simply looking to minimize data latency, mastering these tools is key to optimizing your Snowflake-powered data ecosystem.

Introduction to Data Loading Strategies for Snowflake

Let's look at the traditional way of dealing with loading data into a data warehouse. Figure 3-1 shows data that's being generated continuously, loaded into a staging environment like S3, and then batched daily or hourly into your database.

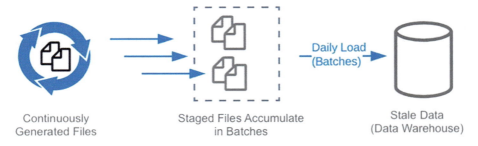

Figure 3-1. *Classical approach to loading into a data warehouse*

Unfortunately, this methodology allows loading data only daily or hourly, or even half-hourly. It does not provide fast access to the data that was generated. Users are often requesting the ability to analyze our data as quickly as it's coming in to make important decisions based on the results being generated.

If you decide to implement a continuous loading system, you're probably aware of the COPY command, which was designed for batch-loading scenarios. After accumulating data over some time, such as hours or days, you can then launch a COPY command to load data into your target table in Snowflake.

> **Note** The COPY command is mainly a SQL command for loading files into a Snowflake table. The command supports different options and file formats. Please see the Snowflake documentation at `https://docs.snowflake.com/en/user-guide/kafka-connector`.

As a workaround for near real-time tasks, you may leverage a micro-batching approach by using the COPY command. It then takes a couple of minutes to use a COPY statement on a schedule to load it. However, it is still not a fully continuous load because fresh data that arrives and is ready for loading into a data warehouse won't be triggered itself. Usually, humans or a scheduler drives it.

If you have data that's being generated continuously, you might think that it'd be great if there were an easily affordable, lightweight way to get your data up-to-date in Snowflake. Luckily, Snowflake agrees with you and created a service called Snowpipe. Snowpipe is an autoscaling Snowflake cloud service that provides continuously loaded data into the Snowflake data warehouse from internal and external stages.

With a continuous loading approach like Snowpipe, you have a data-driven way for new data to arrive from Snowflake to your target table.

Table 3-1 describes the data warehouse loading approaches.

Table 3-1. *Data Warehouse Loading Approaches*

Approach	Definition	Snowpipe Options
Batch	Data accumulates over time (daily, hourly) and is then loaded periodically.	Point at an S3 bucket and a destination table in your warehouse where new data is automatically uploaded.
Microbatch	Data accumulates over small time windows (minutes) and then is loaded.	A technical resource can interface directly using a REST API along with Java and Python SDKs to enable highly customized loading use cases.
Continuously (near real time)	Every data item is loaded individually as it arrives in near real time.	Also available is a way to integrate Apache Kafka using a Kafka connector.

With Snowpipe, you have two options. The first option is to use Snowpipe as an AWS S3 bucket, where you define event notifications on your S3 bucket and then have these event notifications sent to Snowflake as soon as new files land in the S3 bucket. Those files are automatically picked up by Snowpipe and loaded into your target tables.

The second option is to build your own integration with Snowpipe using a REST API. You can create your own applications that call the Snowpipe loader according to your criteria. Table 3-2 is a summary of the critical benefits of using Snowpipe's service.

Table 3-2. *Key Snowpipe Benefits*

Benefits	Description
Continuous loading, immediate insight	Continuously generated data is available for analysis in seconds.
Avoids repeated manual COPY commands, high level of availability for building custom integration	No manual effort is required for loading data into Snowflake.
	Automated loading with no need for manual COPY commands.
	Using a REST API and SDK, you can build your own data pipeline system.
Full support for semi-structured data on load	Availability of many industry-standard formats such as XML, JSON, Parquet, ORC, and Avro.
	No transformation is needed to load varying data types, and there's no trade-off between flexibility and performance.
Pay only for what you use	You pay only for the compute time you use to load data. The "pay only for what you use" pricing model means idle time is not charged for.
	Snowflake's built-for-the-cloud solution scales storage separately from compute, up and down, transparently, and automatically.
	It requires a full understanding of the cost of loading data. There is a separate expense item for "loading data" in your Snowflake bill.
	It has a serverless billing model via utilization-based billing.
Zero management	No indexing, tuning, partitioning, or vacuuming on load.
Serverless	Serverless loading without contention.
	No servers to manage and no impact on other workloads thanks to unlimited concurrency.

CHAPTER 3 CONTINUOUS DATA LOADING WITH SNOWPIPE AND DYNAMIC TABLES

Loading Data Continuously

Let's take a closer look at some options for loading data.

- Snowpipe auto-ingest
- Snowpipe REST API using AWS Lambda

Snowpipe Auto-Ingest

Snowpipe auto-ingest is a fully automatic mode that loads data from the block store into the target table. The speed and ease of configuration provided by using data definition language (DDL) allows any data engineer or analyst to configure their automatic continuous data loading process in minutes.

Figure 3-2 shows the main components of how this integration works.

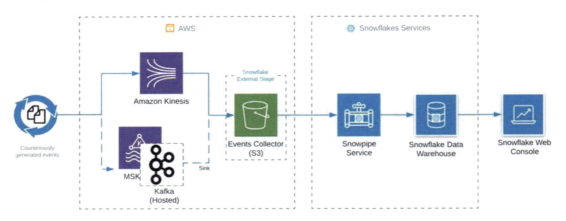

Figure 3-2. *Snowflake continuous data loading approach using Snowpipe with Auto-Ingest*

The data source provides continuous data feeds into services like AWS Kinesis, AWS Managed Streaming for Kafka (MSK), and Hosted Apache Kafka. You can use them to stage your files into an external stage (e.g., S3 bucket) as soon as files arrive in the bucket. S3 sends a notification via an SQS queue to Snowpipe, and as soon as that notification about a new file in the queue is received, Snowpipe runs a serverless loader application that loads the files from S3 into the target tables behind the scenes.

Building a Data Pipeline Using the Snowpipe Auto-Ingest Option

The following components are needed to build an example of a continuously loaded data pipeline.

- Stream Producer, a sample producer for Kinesis Data Firehose (For simplicity, in this case, instead of a stream producer based on the Lambda service, we can use Firehose Test Generator, which is available when creating a Firehose stream.)

- Kinesis Data Firehose as stream delivery service

- S3 bucket as an external Snowflake stage

- The following Snowflake services

    - Snowpipe

    - Snowflake data warehouse

    - Snowflake console

Figure 3-3 shows an overview of the component interaction.

Figure 3-3. *Snowpipe data loading using auto-ingest mode*

CHAPTER 3 CONTINUOUS DATA LOADING WITH SNOWPIPE AND DYNAMIC TABLES

To understand how internal integration actually takes place, we need to dive a little bit into the internal structure of Snowpipe. Figure 3-4 shows the main steps of integration.

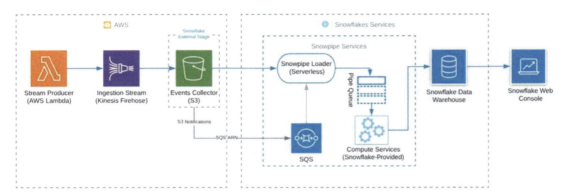

Figure 3-4. *Snowpipe data loading using auto-ingest mode, Snowpipe detail view*

First, we have to create an external *stage* and a *pipe* using the auto_ingest option. When we execute the DDL, we have to get a unique identifier for an internal queue service (with AWS, it is based on SQS) that is already linked to the Snowpipe serverless loader.

Second, we must create a new S3 bucket and configure an S3 bucket event notification that has to send notification events into Snowpipe SNS. The Snowpipe loader gets events about the new file into an S3 bucket and queues pipe statements that contain specific COPY commands. Snowflake computes services fully and automatically scales when executing DDL statements from the pipe queue. The last step is to create and configure a stream that produces intensively a lot of events.

Caution You cannot control transaction boundaries for load with Snowpipe.

BUILDING A DATA PIPELINE USING THE SNOWPIPE AUTO-INGEST OPTION

This exercise builds the pipeline shown in Figure 3-5. Specifically, the following instructions show the process of creating a continuous data pipeline for Snowflake using Snowpipe.

1. Log in to your Snowflake account and choose **Worksheet**.
2. Create Snowflake external stages based on an S3 bucket.

CHAPTER 3   CONTINUOUS DATA LOADING WITH SNOWPIPE AND DYNAMIC TABLES

Replace <your_AWS_KEY_ID> with your AWS credentials, and replace <your_s3_bucket> with your S3 bucket URL.

Run the DDL statements on the worksheet, as shown in the following.

```
-- create a new database for testing snowpipe
create database snowpipe data_retention_time_in_days = 1;
show databases like 'snow%';
-- create a new external stage
create or replace stage snowpipe.public.snowstage
url='S3://<your_s3_bucket>'
credentials=(
AWS_KEY_ID='<your_AWS_KEY_ID>',
AWS_SECRET_KEY='<your_AWS_SEKRET_KEY>');
-- create target table for Snowpipe
create or replace table snowpipe.public.snowtable(
    jsontext variant
);
-- create a new pipe
create or replace pipe snowpipe.public.snowpipe
    auto_ingest=true as
        copy into snowpipe.public.snowtable
        from @snowpipe.public.snowstage
        file_format = (type = 'JSON');
```

Note Variant is a universal semi-structured data type of Snowflake for loading data in formats such as JSON, Avro, ORC, Parquet, or XML. For more information, you can refer to the references given.

Chapter 3 Continuous Data Loading with Snowpipe and Dynamic Tables

The first part of the preceding code creates a new external stage called `snowpipe.public.snowstage` based on an S3 bucket; we provide the URL S3 bucket and the credentials. Additionally, you can set encryption options.

The next step is to define a target table called `snowpipe.public.snowtable` for the data that we want to load continuously. The table takes a variant column as input for the JSON data.

The last part of the script is a definition of a new pipe called `snowpipe.public.snowpipe`. You can see the pipe is set to `auto_ingest=true`, which means that we are using notifications from S3 into SQS to notify Snowflake about newly arrived data that is ready to load. Also, you can see that the pipe wraps a familiar COPY statement that defines the transformations and the data loading operations that we want to perform on the data as it becomes available.

3. Check the correctness of the configuration using the following commands. Using `show` statements, you can see the status of any pipes and stages.

```
-- check exists pipes and stages
show pipes;
show stages;
```

4. Copy the SQS ARN link from the `NotificationChannel` field in the results of the `show pipes` command.

5. Using a simple `select` statement, you can check the count of loaded data.

```
-- check count of rows in target table
select count(*) from snowpipe.public.snowtable
```

6. Log in to your AWS account.

7. Create an AWS S3 bucket called `<accountname>-snowpipebucket`, as shown in Figure 3-5.

CHAPTER 3   CONTINUOUS DATA LOADING WITH SNOWPIPE AND DYNAMIC TABLES

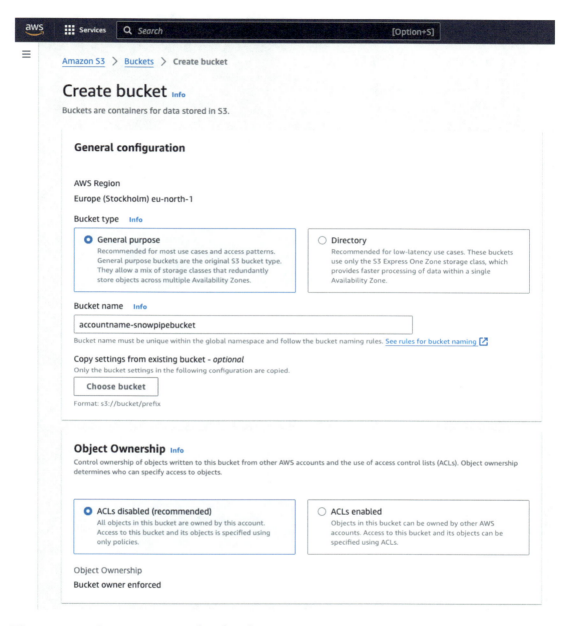

Figure 3-5. *Creating a new bucket for stream events*

8. Set notification events for S3 for Snowpipe using the path S3 ➤ <accountname>-snowpipebucket ➤ Properties ➤ Advanced settings ➤ Events, as shown in Figure 3-6.

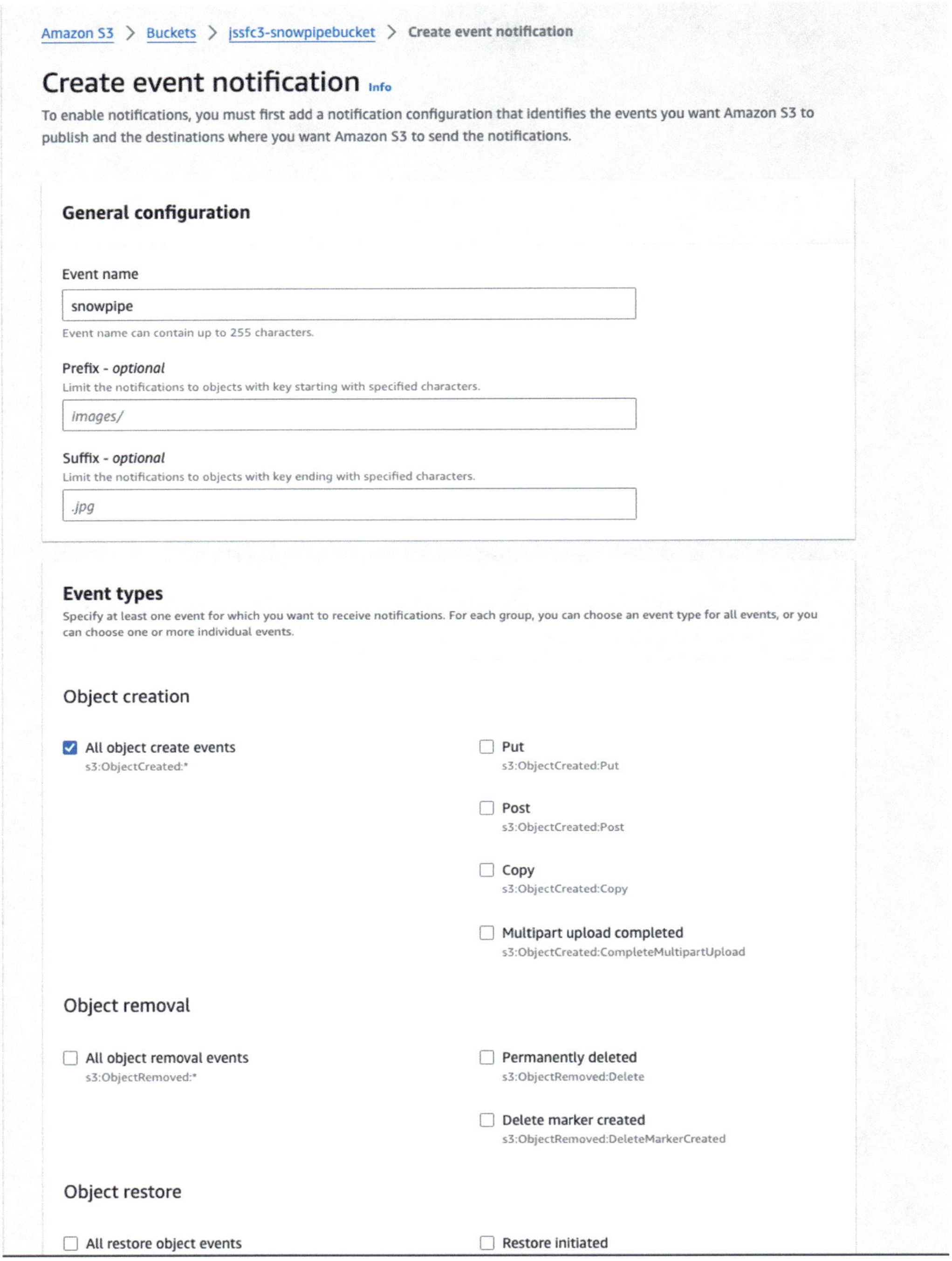

CHAPTER 3   CONTINUOUS DATA LOADING WITH SNOWPIPE AND DYNAMIC TABLES

Figure 3-6. Setting S3 bucket notifications via SQS

CHAPTER 3　CONTINUOUS DATA LOADING WITH SNOWPIPE AND DYNAMIC TABLES

9. Specify the SQS queue, as shown in Figure 3-7.

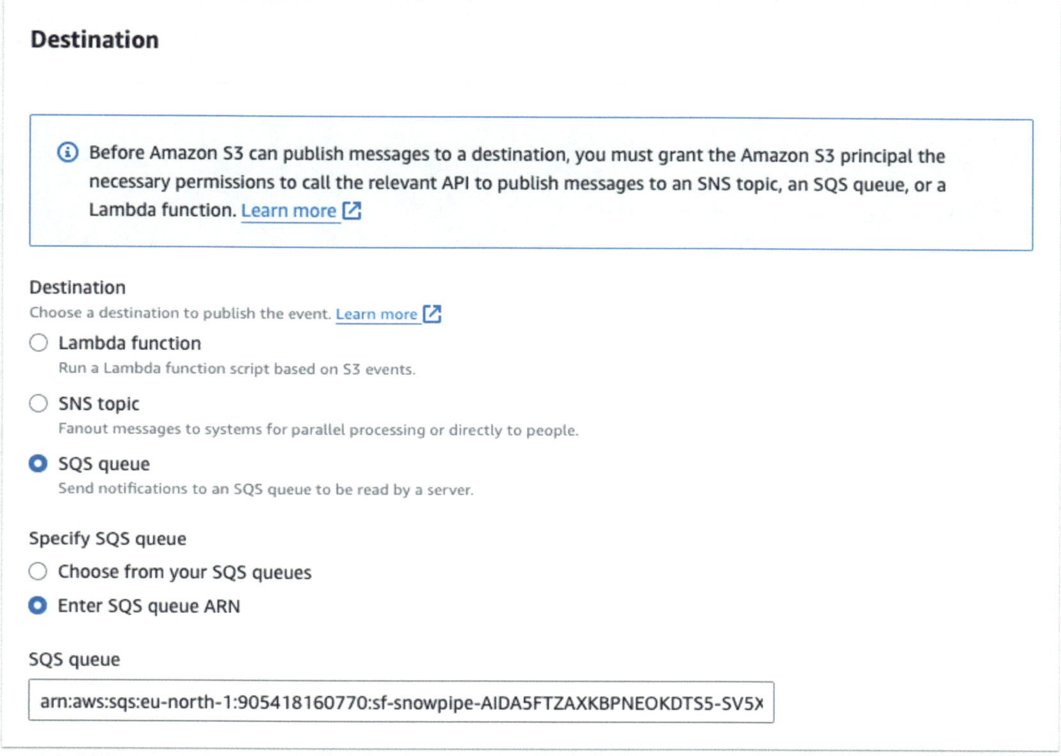

Figure 3-7. Setting S3 bucket notifications via SQS

10. Create a new Kinesis Data Firehose stream using the path Amazon Kinesis ➤ Data Firehose ➤ Create Delivery Stream.

11. Set the source to a direct PUT command, as shown in Figure 3-8.

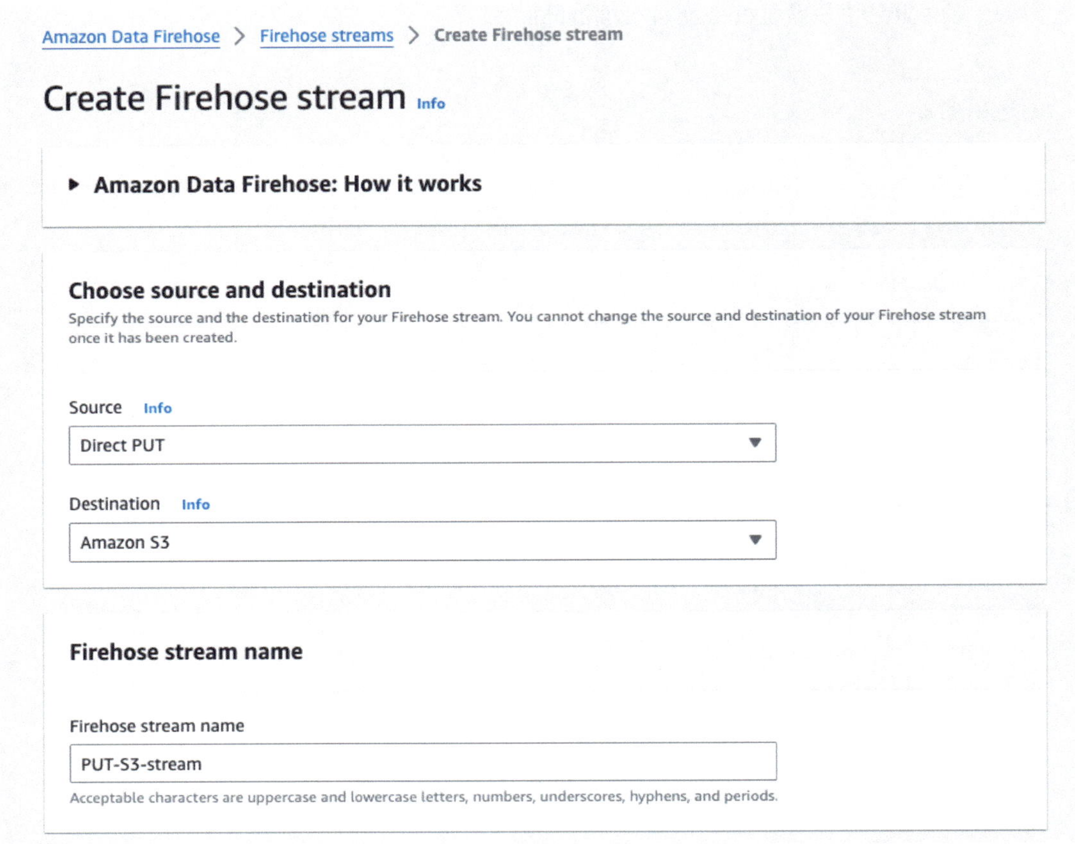

CHAPTER 3   CONTINUOUS DATA LOADING WITH SNOWPIPE AND DYNAMIC TABLES

Figure 3-8.   Creating a new Kinesis Firehose delivery stream

12. Choose a destination for your S3 bucket, as shown in Figure 3-9.

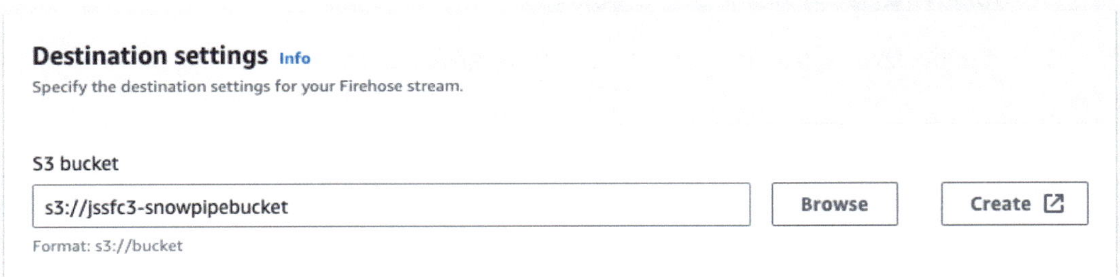

Figure 3-9.   Configuration of Firehose, setting up S3 bucket as the destination

CHAPTER 3 CONTINUOUS DATA LOADING WITH SNOWPIPE AND DYNAMIC TABLES

13. Enable logging using the CloudWatch service, as shown in Figure 3-10.

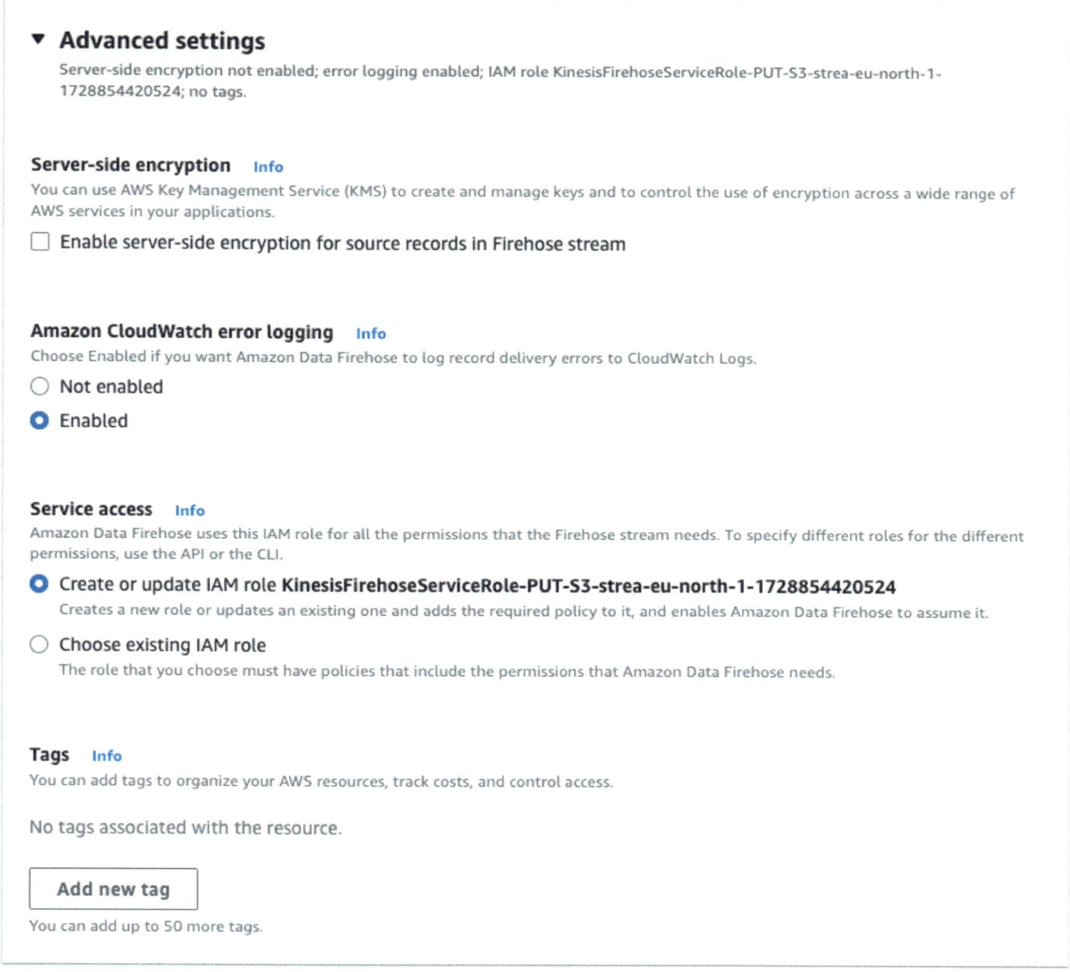

Figure 3-10. Enabling CloudWatch logging

14. Create an IAM role with a policy as follows.

```
...
        {
            "Sid": "",
            "Effect": "Allow",
            "Action": [
                "s3:AbortMultipartUpload",
                "s3:GetBucketLocation",
```

CHAPTER 3 CONTINUOUS DATA LOADING WITH SNOWPIPE AND DYNAMIC TABLES

```
                "s3:GetObject",
                "s3:ListBucket",
                "s3:ListBucketMultipartUploads",
                "s3:PutObject"
            ],
            "Resource": [
                "arn:aws:s3:::snowpipebucket",
                "arn:aws:s3:::snowpipebucket/*",
            ]
        },
    ...
```

15. Run the testing stream, as shown in Figure 3-11.

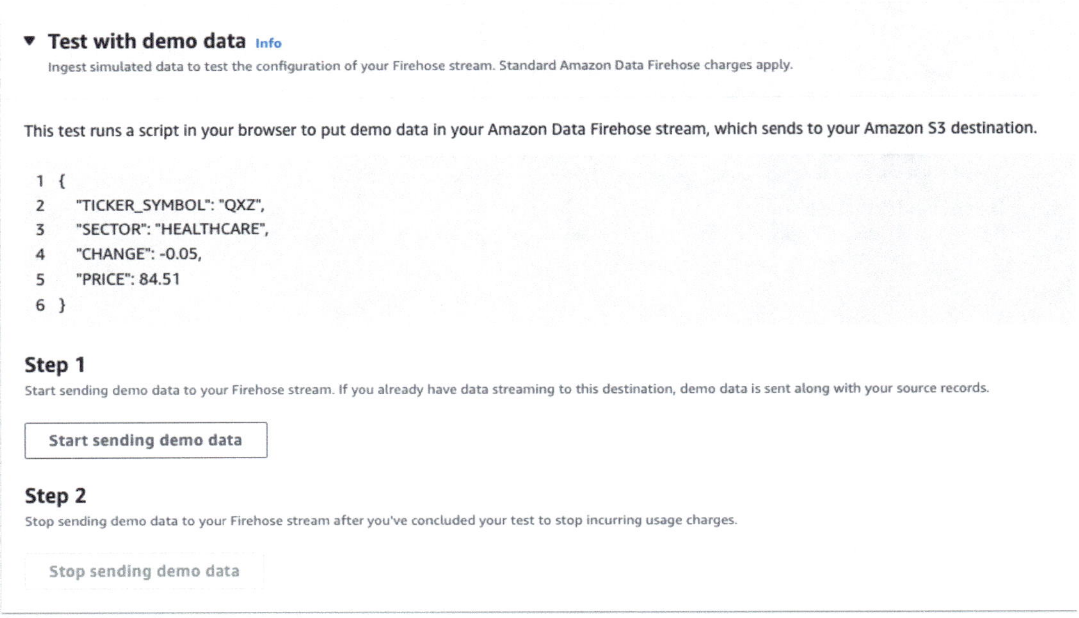

Figure 3-11. Testing

16. Check the file in the S3 bucket.

17. Check the count of loaded data.

```
-- check count of rows in target table
select count(*) from snowpipe.public.snowtable
```

Snowpipe REST API Using AWS Lambda

If the auto-ingest option is not available to your account for some reason, you need a flexible way to integrate with other services so that you can still implement your code through the Snowpipe REST API.

Figure 3-12 shows how to build a pipeline with a custom app using the REST API.

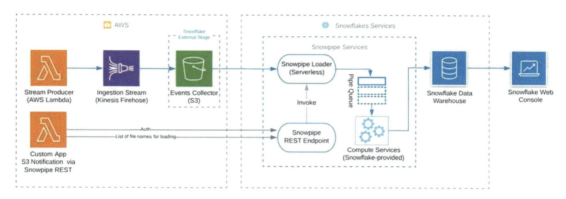

Figure 3-12. *Snowpipe data loading using auto-ingest mode*

Figure 3-12 shows the second option. On the left side, you can see your application. This can be an actual application if you are running one on a virtual machine or a Docker container, but it also can be code that you are running on AWS Lambda. Your Lambda function or application then takes care of placing the load files in the S3 bucket as soon as the file is persisted there.

Snowpipe then adds these files to a queue behind the REST API endpoint. You invoke the REST API, and that invokes the Snowpipe loader service, which works off that queue to load the data into the target tables that you have defined. For step-by-step instructions to do this, you can refer to the official documentation.

CHAPTER 3　CONTINUOUS DATA LOADING WITH SNOWPIPE AND DYNAMIC TABLES

Working with Dynamic Tables in Snowflake

Dynamic tables are a powerful and unique feature in Snowflake that allows continuous and incremental transformations on streaming data. This enables near-real-time data pipelines and faster data processing, reducing the need for batch ETL operations. This recipe dives into how dynamic tables work, how to set them up, and how to integrate them into your Snowflake data architecture.

What Are Dynamic Tables?

In Snowflake, dynamic tables provide a mechanism to automatically and continuously refresh table data based on underlying changes in the source tables. The key feature of dynamic tables is that they manage incremental transformations in a continuous manner without manual intervention or complex orchestration. This makes them particularly useful when working with high-velocity data that requires regular transformations or aggregations.

In essence, dynamic tables allow you to automate the materialization of SQL queries into tables while the system keeps track of changes and updates them as new data flows in. You can think of dynamic tables as a reactive layer in your data architecture, responding to upstream changes without requiring manual refreshes or scheduled batch jobs.

This reactive architecture fits well with Snowflake's event-driven approach to data loading, specifically when used with Snowpipe, to ensure your data is always up to date.

Why Use Dynamic Tables?

Let's briefly go over the benefits of using dynamic tables.

- **Continuous transformations**: Unlike traditional batch processing, where transformations run periodically, dynamic tables ensure your transformations run as soon as the source data is updated. This is ideal for near real-time analytics.

CHAPTER 3   CONTINUOUS DATA LOADING WITH SNOWPIPE AND DYNAMIC TABLES

- **Automatic refresh**: You don't need to schedule jobs or manually refresh the tables. Snowflake keeps them updated by listening to changes in the underlying data.

- **Simplicity**: Instead of writing complex logic to handle incremental data loads, dynamic tables handle the complexity for you, simplifying your data pipelines.

- **Scalability**: They scale automatically with Snowflake's elastic infrastructure, ensuring efficient performance even as data volume grows.

USING DYNAMIC TABLES FOR CONTINUOUS DATA LOADING

Let's walk through the steps to create and use dynamic tables in Snowflake. This example assumes that there is already a data stream being ingested into Snowflake via Snowpipe. It demonstrates how to create a dynamic table that continuously transforms data from a JSON column stored in a table SNOWTABLE created in the first exercise. Our goal is to extract key fields from the JSON data and store them in a new, structured table. Dynamic tables make it easy to set up continuous transformations as data changes or is loaded.

1. Log in to your Snowflake account and choose **Worksheet**.

2. A warehouse is essential because it provides the compute resources to execute queries for dynamic tables. To create a warehouse, you can use the following SQL command.

```sql
-- Creating a Warehouse in Snowflake
CREATE WAREHOUSE IF NOT EXISTS my_warehouse
  WITH
  WAREHOUSE_SIZE = 'XSMALL'
  AUTO_SUSPEND = 300
  AUTO_RESUME = TRUE;
```

Note   WAREHOUSE_SIZE = 'XSMALL': This specifies the size of the warehouse. You can adjust the size (XSMALL, SMALL, MEDIUM, etc.) based on your needs.

CHAPTER 3   CONTINUOUS DATA LOADING WITH SNOWPIPE AND DYNAMIC TABLES

AUTO_SUSPEND = 300 sets the warehouse to automatically suspend (stop) after 5 minutes of inactivity, helping you save costs.

AUTO_RESUME = TRUE allows the warehouse to automatically resume when a query needs to run, avoiding manual intervention.

3. After running the CREATE WAREHOUSE command, verify that the warehouse was actually created. You can check this by running.

   SHOW WAREHOUSES;

4. Next, define the dynamic table that automatically transforms the JSON data and stores it in TRANSFORMED_JSON. Here's how to create the dynamic table using the SQL logic.

```
CREATE OR REPLACE DYNAMIC TABLE transformed_json_table
WAREHOUSE = 'MY_WAREHOUSE'
TARGET_LAG = '5 minutes'
AS
SELECT
    json_key,
    json_value
FROM (
    WITH transformed_json AS (
        SELECT
            JSONTEXT,
            PARSE_JSON(JSONTEXT) AS json_data
        FROM
            SNOWTABLE
    ),
    flattened_json AS (
        SELECT
            t.JSONTEXT,
            f.key AS json_key,
            f.value AS json_value
        FROM
            transformed_json t,
            LATERAL FLATTEN(input => t.json_data) f
    )
```

CHAPTER 3   CONTINUOUS DATA LOADING WITH SNOWPIPE AND DYNAMIC TABLES

```
    SELECT
        json_key,
        json_value
    FROM
        flattened_json
);
```

In this step, we define a dynamic table that automatically queries and transforms data from SNOWTABLE.

Each time new data is loaded into SNOWTABLE, Snowflake updates transformed_json_table.

After AS, there is a SQL query that transforms the JSON column by

- Parsing the JSON string using PARSE_JSON.
- Flattening the JSON structure to extract key-value pairs.

Snowflake dynamic tables process data updates periodically based on the TARGET_LAG setting.

- If TARGET_LAG = '5 minutes', the table refreshes every 5 minutes.
- Lower values (e.g., 1 minute) can provide near real-time updates but may increase compute costs.
- The refresh history can be monitored via Snowsight to check when the table was last updated.

5. Test the dynamic table. Similar to the first exercise in this chapter, you can test the process by uploading a JSON file to the S3 bucket.

6. You may need to catch data in Snowpipe by refreshing it.

    ```
    ALTER PIPE SNOWPIPE REFRESH;
    ```

7. Now, let's validate the results in the dynamic table.

    ```
    -- Query the transformed_json_table
    SELECT * FROM transformed_json_table;
    ```

CHAPTER 3   CONTINUOUS DATA LOADING WITH SNOWPIPE AND DYNAMIC TABLES

In this recipe, you learned how to leverage Snowflake's dynamic tables to automatically transform JSON data stored in SNOWTABLE into a structured format. This example highlights how you can use Snowpipe for continuous data loading and dynamic tables for real-time transformation without manual intervention.

By integrating Snowpipe and dynamic tables, you can build robust, scalable data pipelines that require minimal ongoing management. Dynamic tables allow you to keep your transformations in sync with data ingestion, ensuring that your downstream tables are always up to date.

Summary

This chapter explored the power of Snowpipe for continuous data loading, focusing on how to efficiently build and maintain data pipelines in Snowflake. We covered key features like Snowpipe integrations with cloud storage to enable near-real-time data ingestion, examined billing considerations, and explored various options for managing data ingestion.

In addition, the chapter introduced dynamic tables, a powerful tool for automating incremental transformations on streaming data. We demonstrated how to set up dynamic tables that continuously refresh based on underlying data changes, allowing seamless, real-time data transformations.

The next chapter dives into Snowflake administration, discussing the management of primary Snowflake objects such as warehouses, databases, and roles and how to optimize your Snowflake environment for scalability and performance.

CHAPTER 4

Snowflake Administration and RBAC

Snowflake is a database, and as such, it comes with similar administration features as any other database. It was also the first data warehouse as a service, meaning that end users can minimize administration and maintenance.

This chapter provides an overview of options for managing your Snowflake account, geared primarily to Snowflake administrators. However, it is also useful for end users to understand the key concepts of Snowflake administration and management.

There are several main tasks required of administrators.

- Administering roles and users
- Role-based access control
- Administering account parameters
- Administering databases and warehouses
- Administering data shares
- Administering database objects
- Administering clustered tables

This chapter covers all these topics and shows how it works using our Snowflake demo.

CHAPTER 4   SNOWFLAKE ADMINISTRATION AND RBAC

Administering Roles and Users

Snowflake uses *roles* for managing access and operations. In other words, you can create custom roles with a set of privileges to control the granularity of the access granted. For instance, let's say we want to create a role for our marketing team that grants the team members access to the data and allows them to run SQL queries using a virtual warehouse. According to the Snowflake model, access to securable objects is managed by *privileges* assigned to roles. Moreover, roles can be assigned to other roles and users.

Snowflake now supports flexible hierarchical role structures with multi-level inheritance, allowing complex access patterns to be modeled efficiently. Additionally, dynamic data masking and row access policies provide fine-grained access control tied to roles.

Snowflake leverages the following access control models.

- **Discretionary access control (DAC)**: Each object has an owner, and this owner can manage the access of the object.

- **Role-based access control (RBAC)**: Roles are created and assigned privileges, and then the roles are assigned to users.

A *securable object* is a Snowflake entity to which access can be granted (i.e., database, table, access, and so on). A *privilege* is a level of access to an object.

Figure 4-1 illustrates an example of a marketing role that grants USAGE, MODIFY, and OPERATE privileges to the DATABASE and WAREHOUSE securable objects for marketing users.

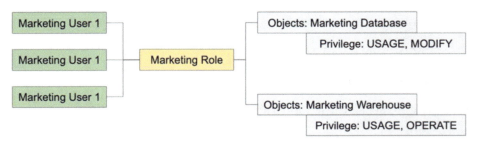

Figure 4-1. *Example of marketing role that is granted specific privileges for marketing users*

When we launched our example Snowflake account, it had several predefined default roles.

- **ACCOUNTADMIN**: This account administrator role is the top-level role for a Snowflake account.

- **SYSADMIN**: This system administrator role is for creating and managing databases and warehouses.

- **PUBLIC**: This is a pseudo-role that can be assigned to any object, but they are all available for all account users.

- **SECURITYADMIN**: This security administrator role is for creating and managing roles and users.

- **USERADMIN:** Dedicated to managing user accounts, including creation, modification, suspension, and deletion of users, as well as managing their authentication settings.

- **ORGADMIN:** Available only in multi-account organizations, this role provides organization-level management capabilities for cross-account features.

To create custom roles, you typically use the **SECURITYADMIN** role, or you can grant the **CREATE ROLE** privilege to another role. Snowflake's role hierarchy should be carefully designed to ensure proper delegation of access and responsibilities. Regular audits of roles can be performed using the **ACCESS_HISTORY** view to ensure compliance with access policies.

Figure 4-2 is an example of this hierarchy. It shows the Marketing role, which has privileges for the marketing database, schema, and warehouse that belong to the SYSADMIN role.

CHAPTER 4 SNOWFLAKE ADMINISTRATION AND RBAC

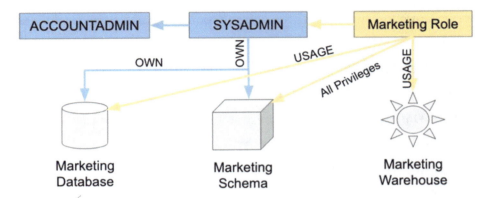

Figure 4-2. *An example of a custom role hierarchy*

Enforcement Model

When you log in to your Snowflake account via the web interface or through ODBC/JDBC clients, a session is initiated. In that session, a current role is automatically set for you. This role determines the permissions you have during that session. You can manually switch to a different role during your session if you have been granted access to multiple roles. It is possible to change the role using the USE ROLE command or to switch roles by using the menu in the top-right corner of the worksheet you work in (see Figure 4-3).

CHAPTER 4 SNOWFLAKE ADMINISTRATION AND RBAC

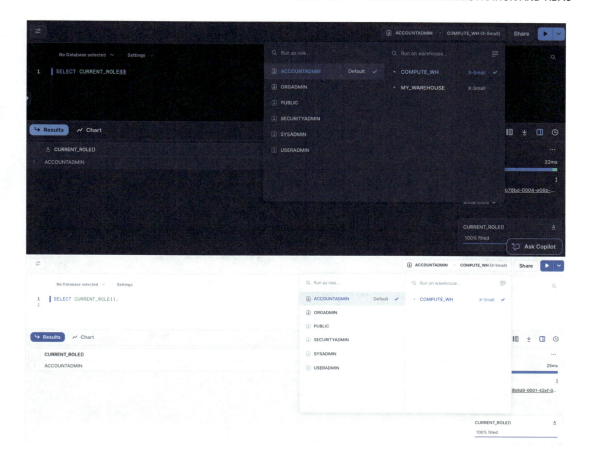

Figure 4-3. *Role switching in the worksheet*

It's also available in the bottom-left corner by clicking the profile icon (see Figure 4-4).

63

CHAPTER 4   SNOWFLAKE ADMINISTRATION AND RBAC

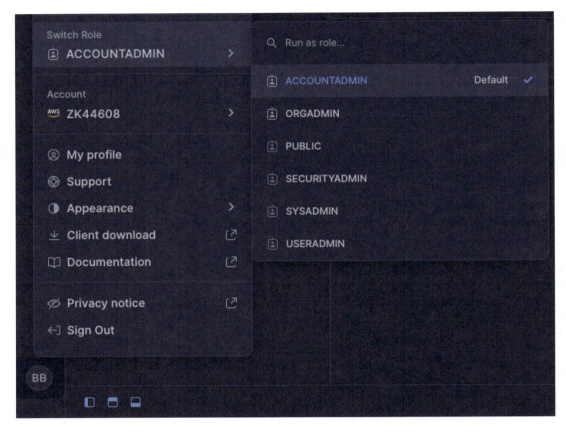

Figure 4-4. Role switching in the profile menu

When a user wants to perform any action in Snowflake, Snowflake compares the user's role privileges against the required privileges.

Note   You may be familiar with the concept of a super-user or super-role with other database vendors, but you do not find this functionality in Snowflake. All access requires the appropriate access privileges.

Secondary Roles

Snowflake supports secondary roles, which allow users to activate multiple roles in a session in addition to their primary role. This feature helps simplify role management and reduces the need for frequent role switching during a session. When secondary roles are enabled, the user can access privileges granted to any of the active roles simultaneously, as long as those roles are assigned to the user. This is particularly useful for scenarios where a user needs to read data from one schema, write to another, and manage tasks—all under different roles. Secondary roles can be activated using the `ALTER SESSION SET SECONDARY_ROLES = ('ALL')` command or a similar configuration.

Working with Roles and Users (with RBAC)

Snowflake allows you to control your data warehouse at a granular level within roles. To create a role, you can execute DDL commands or use the web interface. The following commands are used for role management.

- `CREATE ROLE` creates a new role.
- `ALTER ROLE` modifies an existing role.
- `DROP ROLE` deletes an existing role.
- `SHOW ROLES` displays a list of available roles.
- `USE ROLE` switches the active role for the session.

To create a role, ensure you are logged into your Snowflake account with a role that has the required privileges, such as SECURITYADMIN.

```
CREATE ROLE MARKETING_TEAM;
CREATE ROLE DATA_SCIENCE_TEAM;
```

These commands create two new roles: MARKETING_TEAM for the marketing analysts and DATA_SCIENCE_TEAM for data scientists.

Next, grant permissions for this role and attach users. The following commands are available for managing users.

- `CREATE USER` creates a new user.
- `ALTER USER` modifies an existing user.
- `DESCRIBE USER` describes user details.
- `SHOW PARAMETERS` displays parameters associated with a user.

CHAPTER 4 SNOWFLAKE ADMINISTRATION AND RBAC

In addition, you can specify the following options for users.

- `userProperties` include attributes like password, display name, email, and so on.
- `sessionParams` are options such as default warehouse, namespace, and query timeout settings.

Here's how to create a new user and assign them to the MARKETING_TEAM role.

```
CREATE USER marketing_analyst
    PASSWORD = 'RockYourData'
    COMMENT = 'Marketing Analyst'
    LOGIN_NAME = 'marketing_user1'
    DISPLAY_NAME = 'Marketing_Analyst'
    DEFAULT_ROLE = "MARKETING_TEAM"
    DEFAULT_WAREHOUSE = 'COMPUTE_WH'
    MUST_CHANGE_PASSWORD = TRUE;

GRANT ROLE "MARKETING_TEAM" TO USER marketing_analyst;
```

To allow the MARKETING_TEAM role to run SQL queries, you must grant it the necessary privileges on the virtual warehouse.

```
GRANT USAGE
    ON WAREHOUSE COMPUTE_WH
    TO ROLE MARKETING_TEAM;
```

The MARKETING_TEAM is now able to use the COMPUTE_WH virtual warehouse to run queries but is not able to suspend or resume the warehouse.

```
CREATE USER data_scientist
    PASSWORD = 'SecurePassword'
    COMMENT = 'Data Scientist'
    LOGIN_NAME = 'data_sci_user1'
    DISPLAY_NAME = 'Data_Scientist'
    DEFAULT_ROLE = "DATA_SCIENCE_TEAM"
    DEFAULT_WAREHOUSE = 'COMPUTE_WH'
    MUST_CHANGE_PASSWORD = TRUE;
```

```
GRANT ROLE "DATA_SCIENCE_TEAM" TO USER data_scientist;

    GRANT USAGE
       ON WAREHOUSE COMPUTE_WH
       TO ROLE DATA_SCIENCE_TEAM;

    GRANT OPERATE ON
       WAREHOUSE COMPUTE_WH
       TO ROLE DATA_SCIENCE_TEAM;
```

The DATA_SCIENCE_TEAM can use the warehouse for running queries (USAGE permission), and it can also manage the warehouse, such as suspending and resuming the warehouse (OPERATE permission).

Note COMPUTE_WH is an X-Small virtual warehouse that was created by default, but you can use your own warehouse. For demo purposes, it is always good to use the smallest computing instance.

Again, the web interface can be used to perform the same actions. Then, you can log in with a new user, using `login marketing_user1`, and run this sample query.

```
SELECT * FROM "SNOWFLAKE_SAMPLE_DATA"."TPCH_SF1"."REGION"
```

You can perform all the preceding actions using the Snowflake web interface. To manage roles, users, and permissions, navigate to the **Admin** menu on the left navigation pane, and select the **Users & Roles** tab, as shown in Figure 4-5.

Figure 4-5. Admin Users and Roles menu

By default, the **Admin** menu is available for the ACCOUNTADMIN role. This menu is usually accessible to Snowflake administrators. It allows them to manage users and roles, control credit usage, and so on.

The following describes RBAC best practices.

- **Least privilege**: Always assign users the minimum permissions necessary for their job functions. The MARKETING_TEAM role should only have USAGE permissions, while the DATA_SCIENCE_TEAM role should have more powerful permissions like OPERATE.

- **Role hierarchy**: You can create additional roles that inherit permissions from others. For example, an ADMIN role could inherit all privileges from DATA_SCIENCE_TEAM to manage warehouses at a higher level.

- **Audit**: Regularly review the roles and permissions granted to ensure no one has more access than necessary. Monitor actions performed by users with powerful privileges like OPERATE.

By implementing RBAC, you can ensure that your Snowflake environment is secure and well-organized and that access is tailored to the needs of each user.

New Role Types: Database Roles and Application Roles

In addition to traditional account-level roles, Snowflake now supports database roles and application roles, providing more modular and secure access control. Database roles are scoped to individual databases, enabling more localized privilege management that can be transferred with the database itself—a valuable feature for data product teams or in cross-environment deployments. Application roles are used within Snowflake Native Apps, ensuring that access to app-specific objects is governed independently of account-level roles. These newer role types allow teams to build more reusable, isolated, and secure components within Snowflake, aligning access patterns more closely with modern data architecture practices.

Using Permifrost for RBAC in Snowflake

Permifrost (`https://pypi.org/project/permifrost/`) is an open source tool that simplifies managing and deploying RBAC policies in Snowflake. It allows you to define

CHAPTER 4   SNOWFLAKE ADMINISTRATION AND RBAC

Snowflake roles, users, and permissions declaratively using YAML files and ensures your access control policies are consistent and easy to manage.

Make sure you have the following prerequisites.

- A Snowflake account with an administrative role (SECURITYADMIN or equivalent) to manage roles and permissions.
- Python is installed on your machine (Permifrost is a Python-based tool).
- A Snowflake user account with a Snowflake private key for authentication.

1. Install Permifrost using pip.

   ```
   pip install permifrost
   ```

2. Create a YAML file (e.g., rbac_config.yaml) to define your roles, users, and permissions. Here's an example configuration.

   ```
   roles:
     - name: MARKETING_TEAM
       grants:
         warehouses:
           - name: COMPUTE_WH
             privileges:
               - USAGE
         schemas:
           - name: "SNOWFLAKE_SAMPLE_DATA.TPCH_SF1"
             privileges:
               - USAGE
               - SELECT
     - name: DATA_SCIENCE_TEAM
       grants:
         warehouses:
           - name: COMPUTE_WH
             privileges:
               - USAGE
               - OPERATE
   ```

```yaml
        schemas:
          - name: "SNOWFLAKE_SAMPLE_DATA.TPCH_SF1"
            privileges:
              - USAGE
              - SELECT
    users:
      - name: marketing_analyst
        default_role: MARKETING_TEAM
        roles:
          - MARKETING_TEAM
      - name: data_scientist
        default_role: DATA_SCIENCE_TEAM
        roles:
          - DATA_SCIENCE_TEAM
```

The following are the roles in this configuration.

- MARKETING_TEAM can query the COMPUTE_WH warehouse and access data in the TPCH_SF1 schema.

- DATA_SCIENCE_TEAM has additional permissions to manage (OPERATE) the COMPUTE_WH warehouse.

The following users are in this configuration.

- marketing_analyst is assigned the MARKETING_TEAM role.

- data_scientist is assigned the DATA_SCIENCE_TEAM role.

3. To apply the RBAC policy, execute the following command.

```
permifrost apply --config rbac_config.yaml
```

Permifrost connects to your Snowflake account and ensures the defined roles, users, and permissions are configured correctly.

You can verify the applied RBAC configuration directly in Snowflake.

The following describes the benefits of using Permifrost.

- **Consistency**: All RBAC policies are managed declaratively in a YAML file.

- **Automation**: Simplifies the deployment of roles and permissions across environments.

- Auditability: The YAML file serves as documentation for your RBAC configuration.

- Ease of Use: Avoids manual SQL commands and reduces the risk of errors.

By using Permifrost, managing RBAC in Snowflake becomes streamlined, reproducible, and aligned with best practices for access control.

Dynamic Data Masking

Snowflake is often used to store and process sensitive data, including Personally Identifiable Information (PII) and other confidential business data. Ensuring the security and privacy of this data is critical to maintaining compliance with regulations such as GDPR, CCPA, HIPAA, and internal corporate policies.

The following describes best practices for handling PII and confidential data.

- **Data classification**: Identify and classify sensitive data stored in Snowflake. Use tagging and metadata management to label PII and confidential data appropriately.

- **Access control and role-based security**: Leverage Snowflake's RBAC to ensure only authorized users have access to sensitive data. Use least privilege principles to restrict access.

- **Data masking**: Use dynamic data masking to obfuscate PII from unauthorized users while allowing access for users who require it. Snowflake provides built-in masking policies to enforce this at the column level.

- **Row-level security**: Implement row access policies to ensure users only see data relevant to their roles and responsibilities.

- **Encryption**: Ensure all data is encrypted both in transit and at rest. Snowflake provides built-in AES-256 encryption for data storage and TLS encryption for data movement.

- **Tokenization and anonymization**: For highly sensitive data, consider tokenization or anonymization techniques to replace PII with pseudonyms, reducing risk exposure.

- **Audit logging and monitoring**: Enable Snowflake's Account Usage views and query history logs to monitor access and usage of sensitive data. Consider integrating with external security monitoring solutions.

- **Data retention and purging**: Implement policies for data retention and deletion to ensure compliance with legal and regulatory requirements. Use Time Travel and Fail-Safe features carefully to manage the data lifecycle.

- **Secure data sharing**: When sharing data externally, use Snowflake's Secure Data Sharing feature to control access without transferring raw data. Apply additional restrictions like masking and row access policies.

- **User training and awareness**: Regularly educate employees on data security best practices, ensuring they understand the risks and compliance requirements associated with handling PII and confidential data. Dynamic Data Masking in Snowflake is a security feature that enables organizations to protect sensitive data by dynamically modifying query results based on user roles and permissions. It ensures that unauthorized users only see masked or obfuscated values while authorized users can access full data.

You can use SnowSight to create a masking policy.

```
CREATE MASKING POLICY ssn_masking_policy AS (val STRING) RETURNS STRING ->
CASE WHEN CURRENT_ROLE() IN ('PII_ADMIN', 'DATA_ANALYST') THEN val ELSE
'XXX-XX-XXXX' END;
```

CHAPTER 4　SNOWFLAKE ADMINISTRATION AND RBAC

Next, apply the masking policy to a column(s).

```
ALTER TABLE customers MODIFY COLUMN ssn SET MASKING POLICY ssn_
masking_policy;
```

You can verify the masking policy as follows.

```
SELECT ssn FROM customers;
```

If the current role is not PII_ADMIN or DATA_ANALYST, the output shows masked values (XXX-XX-XXXX). Otherwise, the actual SSN values are displayed. You can learn more about Dynamic Data Masking in Snowflake's official documentation at https://docs.snowflake.com/en/user-guide/security-column-ddm-intro.

Administering Databases and Warehouses

Snowflake provides flexibility in managing databases and virtual warehouses through either the web interface or SQL commands. This section focuses on common administrative actions related to databases and warehouses.

Managing Warehouses

As an administrator, you can use the following commands with warehouses.

- CREATE WAREHOUSE creates a new virtual warehouse.
- DROP WAREHOUSE deletes an existing warehouse.
- ALTER WAREHOUSE modifies the properties of a warehouse, such as size, suspend settings, or other parameters.
- USE WAREHOUSE sets the active warehouse for the current session.

Let's create a new warehouse by executing a command using the ACCOUNTADMIN role.

```
CREATE WAREHOUSE RYD
    WITH WAREHOUSE_SIZE = 'XSMALL'
        WAREHOUSE_TYPE = 'STANDARD'
        AUTO_SUSPEND = 300
        AUTO_RESUME = TRUE
        COMMENT = 'Rock Your Data Virtual Warehouse';
```

The following applies in this example.

- `WAREHOUSE_SIZE = 'XSMALL'` specifies the smallest possible warehouse size.
- `AUTO_SUSPEND` automatically suspends the warehouse after 300 seconds of inactivity.
- `AUTO_RESUME` automatically resumes the warehouse when a query requires it.

You also have an option to resize the warehouse using the `ALTER WAREHOUSE` command. Finally, you can use the `USE WAREHOUSE` command to specify which warehouse to use for the current session.

> **Note** `ALTER WAREHOUSE` is a unique feature. It exists only in Snowflake. This command suspends or resumes a virtual warehouse or aborts all queries (and other SQL statements) for a warehouse. It can also be used to rename or set/unset the properties for a warehouse. There are more details available at https://docs.snowflake.com/en/sql-reference/sql/alter-warehouse.

Managing Databases

In Snowflake, all data is stored in database tables structured as collections of columns and rows. Each database can have one or more schemas, and within schemas, you can create database objects such as tables, views, and more.

> **Note** Snowflake doesn't have a hard limit on the number of databases, schemas, or database objects.

The following are the main commands used to manage databases.

- `CREATE DATABASE` creates a new database.
- `CREATE DATABASE CLONE` creates a zero-copy clone of an existing database.

- ALTER DATABASE modifies database properties.
- DROP DATABASE deletes a database.
- UNDROP DATABASE restores a recently dropped database within the retention window.
- USE DATABASE specifies the active database for the session.
- SHOW DATABASES lists all databases visible to the current role.

These commands could be executed via the web interface of SQL. Let's create a database.

CREATE DATABASE MARKETING_SANDBOX;

You can grant privileges like CREATE SCHEMA, MODIFY, MONITOR, and USAGE to specific roles for database management.

Overall, the operations look similar to traditional databases. However, there are a couple of unique features that are worth mentioning.

UNDROP DATABASE

Let's imagine that you accidentally drop the production database. Restoring it from backup could take at least a day. But not with Snowflake; with UNDROP DATABASE you can instantly restore the most recent version of a dropped database if you are within the defined retention window for that database.

This window is controlled by the DATA_RETENTION_TIME_IN_DAYS parameter, which specifies how long dropped objects (like databases, schemas, and tables) can be recovered. By default, this is set to 1 day, but it can be increased up to 90 days for Enterprise edition accounts or higher.

Zero-Copy Cloning

Another unique feature is *zero-copy cloning*, which creates a snapshot of a database. This snapshot is writable and independent. These types of features are like a "dream come true" for data warehouse DBAs.

There are many situations where people need to copy their database to test or experiment with their data to avoid altering their sensitive production database. However, copying data can be painful and time-consuming because all the data needs to be physically moved from the production database to the database copy. This is extremely expensive because both copies of the data need to be paid for. When a production database gets updates, the database copy becomes stale and requires an update.

Snowflake takes a different approach. It enables you to test and experiment with your data more freely. It allows you to copy databases in seconds. Snowflake doesn't physically copy data. It continues to reference the original data and stores new records only when you update or change the data; therefore, you pay for each unique record only once. Finally, you can use zero-copy cloning with the Time Travel feature.

Figure 4-6 shows an option for cloning a database using the web interface.

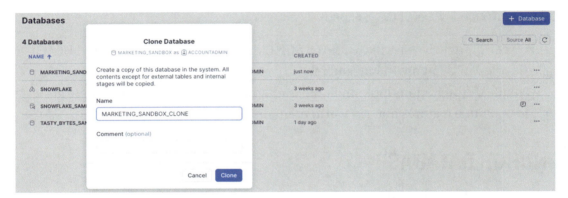

Figure 4-6. *Web interface for cloning a database*

As usual, you have the option to execute a command. The following are examples of commands with definitions.

```
-- Clone a database and all objects within the database at its
current state:

CREATE DATABASE mytestdb_clone
CLONE mytestdb;

-- Clone a schema and all objects within the schema at its current state:

CREATE SCHEMA mytestschema_clone
CLONE testschema;

-- Clone a table at its current state:
```

```
CREATE TABLE orders_clone
CLONE orders;

-- Clone a schema as it existed before the date and time in the specified
timestamp:

CREATE SCHEMA mytestschema_clone_restore
CLONE testschema BEFORE (TIMESTAMP => DATEADD(DAY, -7, CURRENT_TIMESTAMP));

-- Clone a table as it existed exactly at the date and time of the
specified timestamp:

CREATE TABLE orders_clone_restore
CLONE orders AT (TIMESTAMP => TO_TIMESTAMP_TZ('04/05/2023 01:02:03',
'MM/DD/YYYY HH24:MI:SS'));
```

Administering Account Parameters

Parameters in Snowflake control the behavior of the account, individual user sessions, and specific objects. These parameters can be categorized into three types.

- **Account parameters**: Set at the account level and apply globally.
- **Sessions parameters (majority)**: Set at the session, user, or account level; they usually affect query execution and session behavior.
- **Object parameters**: Set for specific objects, such as databases and warehouses, or at the account level for broader control.

To override the default parameters, you can use the following commands.

- ALTER ACCOUNT modifies account-level parameters.
- ALTER SESSION adjusts parameters for the current session.
- CREATE <object> or ALTER <object> sets parameters for objects during creation or modification.

To see the available parameters and their options, run the following.

```
show parameters;
```

Moreover, you can look at the parameters for a specific database or warehouse.

The following are some examples of parameters.

- `STATEMENT_TIMEOUT_IN_SECONDS` specifies the amount of time after which a running SQL statement is canceled by the system. It prevents runaway or resource-intensive queries.

  ```
  ALTER SESSION SET STATEMENT_TIMEOUT_IN_SECONDS = 300; -- 5 minutes
  ```

- `MAX_CONCURRENCY_LEVEL` sets the maximum number of concurrent SQL statements that can execute in a warehouse cluster. It controls workload concurrency.

  ```
  ALTER WAREHOUSE my_warehouse SET MAX_CONCURRENCY_LEVEL = 10;
  ```

- `TIMEZONE` specifies the time zone setting for the session. It controls the time zone for timestamp-related operations.

  ```
  ALTER SESSION SET TIMEZONE = 'Europe/Lisbon';
  ```

Administering Database Objects

One of the most common administration tasks within Snowflake is to manage database objects such as tables, views, schemas, stages, file formats, and so on.

All database objects are created under the schema. Traditional database objects such as tables, views, materialized views, and sequences have similar options.

- `CREATE` creates an object.
- `ALTER` modifies an existing object.
- `DROP` deletes an object.
- `SHOW` lists details of objects.
- `DESCRIBE` views detailed metadata of an object.

Moreover, a Snowflake administrator may leverage Snowflake's unique capabilities like UNDROP and zero-copy cloning.

Another set of schema-level objects that are used in Snowflake include the following.

- **Stage** is used for storing data files, either internally (within Snowflake) or externally (in cloud storage like S3 or Azure Blob Storage).

  ```
  CREATE STAGE my_stage URL='s3://my-bucket/data/' CREDENTIALS=(AWS_
  KEY_ID='key' AWS_SECRET_KEY='secret');
  ```

- **File format** specifies the structure of files for data loading or unloading.

  ```
  CREATE FILE FORMAT my_format TYPE = 'CSV' FIELD_OPTIONALLY_
  ENCLOSED_BY = '"';
  ```

- **Pipe** automates data loading using Snowpipe, allowing continuous ingestion.

  ```
  CREATE PIPE my_pipe AS COPY INTO my_table FROM @my_stage FILE_
  FORMAT = (FORMAT_NAME = my_format);
  ```

- **UDF** allows the creation of custom functions using SQL or JavaScript.

  ```
  CREATE FUNCTION my_udf(x INT) RETURNS INT LANGUAGE SQL AS 'x * 2';
  ```

As a Snowflake administrator, you may need to manage these objects.

Administering Data Shares

Secure Data Sharing is a unique Snowflake feature enabling seamless data sharing without copying data. Administrators can become data providers by creating shares using the following commands.

- CREATE SHARE creates a new share.
- ALTER SHARE modifies an existing share.
- DROP SHARE deletes a share.
- DESCRIBE SHARE views share details.
- SHOW SHARES lists available shares.

CHAPTER 4 SNOWFLAKE ADMINISTRATION AND RBAC

> **Note** As a share creator, you are responsible for data security. Before you create a share, you should spend some time learning more about data and use cases to prevent the sharing of sensitive data. Secure views and UDFs are handy to use when creating shares.

After share creation, an admin can view, grant, or revoke access to database objects using the following commands.

- GRANT <privilege> TO SHARE gives access to an object for a share.
- REVOKE <privilege> TO SHARE removes access from an object for a share.
- SHOW GRANTS TO SHARE displays all object privileges granted to a share.
- SHOW GRANTS OF SHARE lists all accounts using the share or consuming shared data.

In some cases, if you don't need to share anymore and want to drop it, you should consider the downstream impact for all consumers. As an option, you may revoke grants on some objects and see the result.

Administering Clustered Tables

Snowflake, as a data warehouse as a service, simplifies operations by automatically handling aspects like data distribution, sorting, and table statistics.

One aspect of Snowflake's performance is micro-partitioning. When loading data into Snowflake, it is automatically divided into micro-partitions with 50 MB to 500 MB of compressed data. These micro-partitions are organized in a columnar fashion. In addition, Snowflake collects and stores metadata in micro-partitions. This helps to optimize query plans and improve query performance by avoiding unnecessary scanning of micro-partitions through an operation known as *partition pruning*.

Snowflake also stores data in tables and tries to sort it along natural dimensions such as date and/or geographic regions. This is called *data clustering*, and it is a key factor for query performance. It is important, especially for large tables. By default, Snowflake uses automatic clustering. However, in some cases, you may define the clustering key within the CREATE TABLE statement to change the default behavior. This should be an exception rather than a rule. In most cases, admins do not need to cluster. The best practice is to avoid clustering unless there is a specific query pattern that does not meet the SLA. In general, you should not need to cluster unless the table is at least 1 TB.

As a Snowflake administrator, you may need to review table clustering and run reclustering processes to identify all the problem tables and provide the best possible performance.

There are two system functions that allow you to monitor clustering information for tables.

- SYSTEM$CLUSTERING_DEPTH calculates the average depth of clustering for a table.

- SYSTEM$CLUSTERING_INFORMATION provides detailed clustering metrics, including depth, for a specific table.

If you need to improve the clustering of data, you should create a new table with a new clustering key and insert data into the new table, or you can use materialized views to create a version of the table with the new cluster key. Then, the materialized view function automatically keeps data in sync with the new data added to the base table.

Note A table with clustering keys defined is considered to be clustered. Clustering keys aren't important for all tables. Whether to use clustering depends on the size of a table and the query performance, and it is most suitable for multi-terabyte tables.

Snowflake Materialized Views

According to Snowflake, a *materialized view* is a precomputed dataset derived from a query specification (SELECT in the view definition) and stored for later use. Because the data is precomputed, querying a materialized view is faster than executing the original query. This performance difference can be significant when a query is run frequently or is sufficiently complex.

Note Materialized views are designed to improve query performance for workloads composed of common, repeated query patterns. However, materializing intermediate results incur additional costs. As such, before creating any materialized views, you should consider whether the costs are offset by the savings from reusing these results frequently.

There are a couple of use cases when you can benefit from using materialized views.

- The query results contain a small number of rows and/or columns relative to the base table (the table on which the view is defined).
- The query results require significant processing, including the following.
  - Analysis of semi-structured data (e.g., JSON, Avro)
  - Aggregates that take a long time to calculate

The main benefit of Snowflake materialized views is that they solve the issues of traditional ones. They are views that are automatically maintained by Snowflake. There is a background service that updates them after changes are made to the base table. This is more efficient and less error-prone than manually maintaining the equivalent of a materialized view at the application level.

Table 4-1 shows the key similarities and differences between tables, regular views, cached query results, and materialized views.

Table 4-1. Key Similarities and Differences

	Performance Benefits	Security Benefits	Simplifies Query Logic	Supports Clustering	Uses Storage	Uses Credits for Maintenance
Regular table				👍	👍	
Regular view		👍	👍			
Cached query result	👍					
Materialized view	👍	👍	👍	👍	👍	👍

Summary

This chapter covered the main Snowflake administrative duties (e.g., user and role administration), RBAC, and Permifrost, and you learned about key Snowflake objects (e.g., warehouses and schema-level objects). The chapter also reviewed billing and usage information and discussed data shares, data clustering concepts, and materialized views.

The next chapter discusses one of the key elements of cloud analytics: security.

CHAPTER 5

Secure Data Sharing

In today's interconnected world, secure and efficient data sharing is paramount for modern businesses. The ability to seamlessly exchange data within and outside an organization unlocks a wealth of opportunities for collaboration, innovation, and informed decision-making. Yet, traditional data sharing methods often present significant challenges, including cumbersome data transfers, security risks, and the burden of maintaining data consistency across multiple systems.

This chapter delves into the realm of secure data sharing, exploring the innovative features offered by Snowflake that revolutionize the data sharing landscape by enabling seamless and secure data exchange between different accounts within a region. We embark on a comprehensive journey to unravel the intricacies of Snowflake's data sharing capabilities, empowering you with the knowledge and tools to leverage this transformative technology.

The chapter covers a range of essential topics.

- **The benefits of Snowflake data sharing**: We begin by examining the compelling advantages of using Snowflake for data sharing, highlighting its speed, security, and flexibility.

- **Understanding share objects**: The concept of "share objects" lies at the heart of Snowflake's data sharing architecture. We explore the role of share objects in defining permissions and granting access to specific database objects.

- **Implementing secure table sharing**: We provide a step-by-step guide to sharing tables securely using Snowflake, including creating share objects, granting privileges, and accessing shared data.

- **Leveraging secure views for granular control**: Secure views empower data providers with fine-grained control over shared data. We delve into the process of creating secure views and using them to implement row-level access control.

CHAPTER 5   SECURE DATA SHARING

By the end of this chapter, you should have a solid grasp of Snowflake's secure data sharing features and be equipped to harness their power to foster seamless collaboration and unlock the full potential of your data assets.

Benefits of Snowflake Data Sharing

Snowflake's data sharing capabilities offer a compelling alternative to traditional data sharing methods, providing several key benefits for businesses.

- **No data movement, no data copying**: First and foremost, Snowflake eliminates the need for *data movement or copying*. With traditional methods, sharing data often involves extract-transform-load (ETL) processes, leading to data duplication and potential inconsistencies. Snowflake's approach avoids these complexities by enabling data consumers to access shared data directly in the provider's environment without physically transferring the data.

- **Instant access to data**: This approach not only streamlines the data sharing process but also ensures that consumers always access the most up-to-date information as updates made by the provider are instantly reflected.

- **Security**: Snowflake prioritizes security. While methods like FTP or email exchange can pose security risks, Snowflake's secure data sharing model allows providers to grant limited access to specific objects such as tables, secure views, or user-defined functions (UDFs).

- **Access control**: Secure views play a crucial role in providing row-level access control, ensuring that consumers only see the data they are authorized to access. This granular control over data visibility enhances security and protects sensitive information.

Understanding Share Objects

Having established the numerous advantages Snowflake data sharing offers, let's delve into the mechanism that makes this seamless and secure exchange possible. At the heart of Snowflake's data sharing architecture lies share objects. These objects play a pivotal role in defining how data is shared and accessed between different Snowflake accounts within a region.

It is important to understand that in the process of sharing, there is no real copying of data. Therefore, the data consumer pays only for the computing service but does not pay for the storage of this data since, physically, the data remains stored with the data provider. Since the information is not actually transferred, consumers get an instant update when the provider changes the data. A single data provider may have multiple data consumers, both within the company and with external consumers. Similarly, data consumers may have access to multiple providers, thereby forming a network of providers and consumers.

The data sharing feature provides the ability to share database objects between Snowflake's accounts within a region by using a specific share object. Such objects can be tables, secure views, and secure UDFs. The data provider first creates a share object, which is a named Snowflake object that encapsulates information to share between the provider and consumer, such as the following.

- Permissions that allow access to the **provider**'s database and selected objects.
- **Consumer** database and objects that are shared.

The data sharing feature in Snowflake works only between Snowflake accounts. If you want to grant access to the outside world, you need to use a *reader account*. A provider account can create reader accounts for those consumers who are not customers of Snowflake (see Figure 5-1).

CHAPTER 5 SECURE DATA SHARING

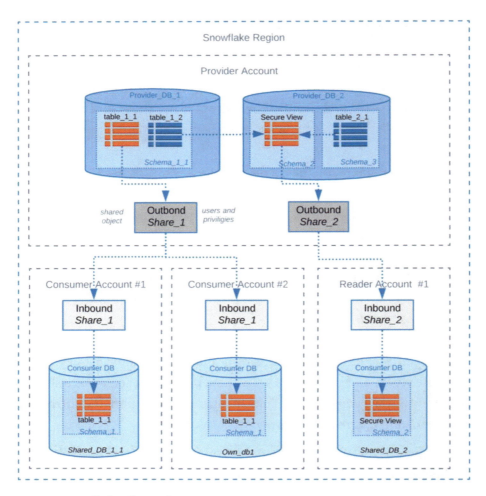

Figure 5-1. *Snowflake data sharing*

Table 5-1 highlights the steps of the data sharing process in Figure 5-1.

Table 5-1. *Data Sharing Process*

Step	Description
1	The provider account creates a share object called `Share_1` on the database `Provider_DB_1` and grants access to selected objects in `table_1_1`.
2	The consumer account creates the read-only database from the `Share_1` object. Then, all shared objects are available to consumers. In Figure, the accounts are called Customer Account #1 and Customer Account #2.
3	If consumers do not have an account in Snowflake, the provider can create a reader account for them. In Figure 5-x, this is implemented for the `Share_2` object.
4	Shared objects can be a table (like `table_1_1`), but the best practice is to use a secure view. A view can include multiple private tables from various databases.
5	In a secure view, as an option, you can use control data access by rows. For this, you must create a table in which there is a mapping of a group of records on users.
6	The consumer account grants permissions according to role-based access control.

For more information on reader accounts, see `https://docs.snowflake.net/manuals/user-guide/data-sharing-reader-create.html`.

Implementing Secure Table Sharing

If you have a table, then to organize access to the table, you need to perform the following steps.

1. Create a share object.

2. Add a table name to the share and grant privileges.

3. Add a consumer account to the share object.

4. Log in to a consumer account.

5. Add the available share to the account, and then you're able to query the share table.

CHAPTER 5 SECURE DATA SHARING

CREATE AND SHARE A TABLE

Let's look at how to share a table in practice by executing the code given in each step.

1. Log in to your Snowflake provider account.

2. Open a blank worksheet and run the following code.

   ```
   -- Create a new database called samples and a schema
   called finance
   use role sysadmin;
   create database samples;
   create schema samples.finance;

   -- Create a table named stocks_data in the samples.
   finance schema
   create or replace table samples.finance.stocks_data (
       id int,
       symbol string,
       date date,
       time time(9),
       bid_price float,
          ask_price float,
          bid_cnt int,
          ask_cnt int
   );

   -- Insert values into your stocks_data table.
   insert into samples.finance.stocks_data
    values(1,'TDC',dateadd(day,  -1,current_date()), '10:15:00',
   36.3, 36.0, 10, 10),
    (2,'TDC', dateadd(month,-2,current_date()), '11:14:00', 36.5,
   36.2, 10, 10),
    (3,'ORCL', dateadd(day, -1,current_date()), '11:15:00',57.8,
   59.9, 13, 13),
    (4,'ORCL', dateadd(month,-2,current_date()), '09:11:00',57.3,
   57.9, 12, 12),
   ```

```
        (5,'TSLA', dateadd(day, -1,current_date()), '11:01:00', 255.2,
        256.4, 22, 22),
        (6,'TSLA', dateadd(month, -2,current_date()), '11:13:00', 255.2,
        255.7, 23, 23);
        select * from samples.finance.stocks_data;
```

ROWID	SYMBOL	DATE	TIME	BID_PRICE	ASK_PRICE	BID_CNT	ASK_CNT
1	TDC	2019-07-18	10:15:00	36.3	36	10	10
2	TDC	2019-05-19	11:14:00	36.5	36.2	10	10
3	ORCL	2019-07-18	11:15:00	57.8	59.9	13	13
4	ORCL	2019-05-19	09:11:00	57.3	57.9	12	12
5	TSLA	2019-07-18	11:01:00	255.2	256.4	22	22
6	TSLA	2019-05-19	11:13:00	255.2	255.7	23	23

Figure 5-2. *The output of the samples.finance.stocks table after running the code in step 2*

3. Run the following code. It creates a share object and grant permissions to a new account.

```
# Create and show share. Figure 5-3 shows how this displays
use role accountadmin;

create or replace share stocks_share;
show shares;
```

```
#Provide permissions on database samples and add to the
stocks_share share grant usage on database samples to share
stocks_share;
```

```
#Provide permissions to finance schema and add to the stocks_
share share grant usage on schema samples.finance to share
stocks_share;
```

```
#Provide permissions on stocks_data table and add to the stocks_
share share.
grant select on table samples.finance.stocks_data to share
stocks_share;
```

CHAPTER 5 SECURE DATA SHARING

```
# Display the objects granted to stocks_share. Figure 5-4 shows how
this should look show grants to share stocks_share;

# Add consumer access to the stocks_share for the <consumer_account>
alter share stocks_share add accounts=<consumer_account>;
```

Row	↓ created_on	kind	name	database_name	to	owner	comment
3	2019-07-17 17:0...	OUTBOUND	⌘⌘⌘.STOCKS_SHARE	SAMPLES		ACCOUNTADMIN	

Figure 5-3. *Metadata of share object*

created_on	privilege	granted_on	name	granted_to	grantee_name	grant_option	granted_by
2019-07-17 ...	USAGE	DATABASE	SAMPLES	SHARE	⌘⌘⌘.STOCKS_SHARE	false	SYSADMIN
2019-07-17 ...	USAGE	SCHEMA	SAMPLES.FINANCE	SHARE	⌘⌘⌘.STOCKS_SHARE	false	SYSADMIN
2019-07-17 ...	SELECT	TABLE	SAMPLES.FINANCE.STOCKS_DATA	SHARE	⌘⌘⌘.STOCKS_SHARE	false	SYSADMIN

Figure 5-4. *Grants on a share object*

4. Show the available share in the consumer account by running this code

   ```
   use role accountadmin;
   show shares;
   desc share <consumer_account>.STOCKS_SHARE;
   ```

Figure 5-5. *The available shares in consumer account*

5. Log in to the <consumer_account> used in the previous steps for grants and create a database based on the share by running this code. Once you've executed the code, you can see shared_db from the Snowsight UI, as shown in Figure 5-6.

   ```
   create database shared_db from share <provider_account>.
   STOCKS_SHARE;
   ```

CHAPTER 5 SECURE DATA SHARING

```
SHARED_DB
  FINANCE
    ▼ Tables
        STOCKS_DATA
    No Views in this Schema
```

Figure 5-6. *Available shared objects in the consumer account*

6. Query the shared table from the database you created previously. Figure 5-7 shows the results.

```
select * from SHARED_DB.Finance.STOCKS_DATA;
```

Figure 5-7. *The results after querying the shared table*

Data Sharing Using a Secure View

Often, there is a situation where you have a base table, and you need to organize access to only part of the records of this table. The best practice is to use **secure views**. If you have a table, you need to perform these steps to organize access to the table within a secure view.

6. If needed, add a new column to a table to be able to filter data into meaningful groups.

7. Create a mapping table to track the name of the groups and the name of the consumer Snowflake account.

93

CHAPTER 5 SECURE DATA SHARING

   8. Create a secure view of the table.

   9. Create a share object.

   10. Add the secure view to the share object and grant appropriate privileges.

   11. Add the consumer Snowflake account to the share object.

Note Step 1 may not be needed if your table already has a column where filtering the data can be accomplished. For example, if your table has a region column and you want to only share specific region data in your share object, you can use that column.

SHARING A TABLE USING A SECURE VIEW

Let's look at how to provide access row-level sharing using a secure view.

1. Log in to your Snowflake account.

2. Switch to a worksheet and execute the following code to add a grouping column to the stocks_data table.

```
/* Add a grouping column to the stocks_data table. */
use role sysadmin;
alter table samples.finance.stocks_data
  add column access_id string;

/* Updating the grouping column with appropriate grouping data
based on how you want to share the data. In this example we
divided the stock data into two groups, GRP_1 (for sharing with
IT companies) and GRP_2 (for sharing with auto companies). */
update finance.stocks_data
    set access_id = 'GRP_1'
where id in (1,2,3,4);
update finance.stocks_data
    set access_id = 'GRP_2'
```

```
where id in (5,6);

/* Don't forget to commit the changes */
commit;

/* See your changes */
select * from samples.finance.stocks_data;
```

ROWID	SYMBOL	DATE	TIME	BID_PRICE	ASK_PRICE	BID_CNT	ASK_CNT	ACCESS_ID
1	TDC	2019-07-18	10:15:00	36.3	36	10	10	GRP_1
2	TDC	2019-05-19	11:14:00	36.5	36.2	10	10	GRP_1
3	ORCL	2019-07-18	11:15:00	57.8	59.9	13	13	GRP_1
4	ORCL	2019-05-19	09:11:00	57.3	57.9	12	12	GRP_1
5	TSLA	2019-07-18	11:01:00	255.2	256.4	22	22	GRP_2
6	TSLA	2019-05-19	11:13:00	255.2	255.7	23	23	GRP_2

Figure 5-8. *The output of how the changes look after running the code in step 2*

3. Use the following code to create a mapping table for tracking which Snowflake account has access to which access_id.

```
# Create a mapping table to track access_id to Snowflake
consumer account
use role sysadmin;
create or replace table samples.finance.access_map (
  access_id string,
  account string
);
# add access to tech companies for my account
insert into samples.finance.access_map values('GRP_1', current_
account());
# add access to auto companies for my account
insert into samples.finance.access_map values('GRP_2',
'<consumer_account>');
commit;
select * from samples.finance.access_map;
```

CHAPTER 5 SECURE DATA SHARING

4. Create a secure view and apply the appropriate permissions. We used the current_account() function to dynamically identify the user account.

   ```
   # Create a new public schema.
   create or replace schema samples.public;

   # Create a secure view called samples.public.stocks which based
   on the table and the mapping table.
   create or replace secure view samples.public.stocks as
       select sd.symbol, sd.date, sd.time, sd.bid_price, sd.ask_
   price, sd.bid_cnt, sd.ask_cnt
       from samples.finance.stocks_data sd
       join samples.finance.access_map  am on sd.access_id =
   am.access_id
         and am.account = current_account();

   # Grant the appropriate rights to the view
   grant select on samples.public.stocks  to public;
   ```

5. Test access to the table and the secure view.

   ```
   select count(*) from samples.finance.stocks_data;
   select * from samples.finance.stocks_data;
   select count(*) from samples.public.stocks;
   select * from samples.public.stocks;
   select * from samples.public.stocks
   where symbol = 'TDC';
   ```

6. Test the access to the table and secure it by using the session parameter simulated data sharing consumer.

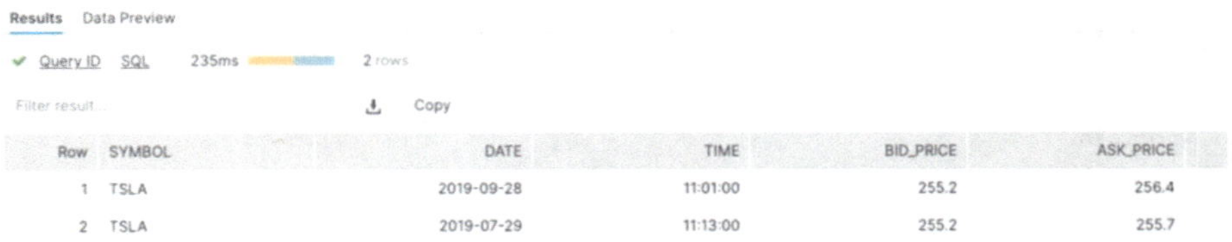

Figure 5-9. *The data of the secure view available to the consumer (in session simulated mode)*

CHAPTER 5 SECURE DATA SHARING

```
alter session set simulated_data_sharing_
consumer=<consumer_name>;
select * from samples.public.stocks;
```

7. Create a share object. Add the secure view and grant privileges.

```
# Return back to the Producer account session
alter session set simulated_data_sharing_consumer='<provider_
account>';
use role accountadmin;

# Create new share object called share_sv
create or replace share share_sv;

# Grant privileges to share object, schema, and view
grant usage on database samples to share share_sv;
grant usage on schema samples.public to share share_sv;
grant select on samples.public.stocks to share share_sv;
show grants to share share_sv;

# grant privileges to share with the consumer accounts
alter share share_sv set accounts = <consumer_accounts>;
show shares;
```

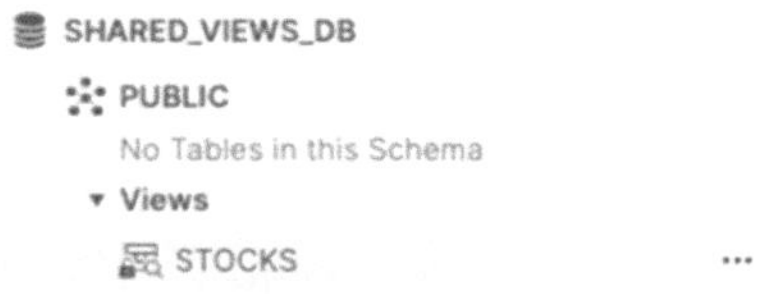

Figure 5-10. The view available for the consumer

8. On the consumer account, create a database from the share object share_sv and grant appropriate privileges.

```
# Create a database from the share object called share_sv.
use role accountadmin;
show shares;
create database shared_views_db from share <provider_account>.
share_sv;
```

```
# Grant import privileges to the share object to sysadmin
grant imported privileges on database shared_views_db to
sysadmin;
use role sysadmin;

# check to ensure access has been granted.
show views;
use warehouse <warehouse_name>;
select * from stocks;
```

Figure 5-11. The data of the secure view available to the consumer

Sharing Regular View vs. Materialized View

In Snowflake, *views* provide a way to simplify and customize data access. A regular view is essentially a stored query. It doesn't store the result set and instead acts as a virtual table that executes the underlying query against the base tables every time it's queried. This ensures that regular views always reflect the most current data. In contrast, a materialized view stores the result set of the query as a physical table. This pre-computed data is automatically maintained and updated by Snowflake when changes occur in the underlying base tables.

Materialized views offer significantly faster query performance, especially for complex or frequently accessed data, but introduce a slight delay in data freshness as they are not updated instantaneously. Therefore, the choice between regular and materialized views depends on the specific needs of the application, balancing the need for up-to-the-minute data with the importance of query performance.

CHAPTER 5 SECURE DATA SHARING

Note Both regular views and materialized views can be defined as "secure." Secure views provide an extra layer of security by preventing consumers from seeing the underlying query definition or accessing the base tables directly, even with direct queries. This is crucial for protecting sensitive data or intellectual property.

In summary, the choice between sharing regular views and materialized views depends on your specific needs and priorities regarding performance, data freshness, and cost considerations. Understanding these differences allows you to make informed decisions about how to best leverage Snowflake's data sharing capabilities. Table 5-2 can help you determine which view type is best for your situation.

Table 5-2. Regular Views vs. Materialized Views

Feature	Regular View	Materialized View
Shared Object	Query definition	Pre-computed data
Data Source	Provider's base tables (queried in real-time)	Stored results set on the provider's side
Performance	Can be slower	Generally faster
Data Freshness	Always up-to-date	May have a short delay in updates
Cost Impact	Primarily consumer compute costs	Provider storage and maintenance costs

Summary

This chapter covered the Snowflake data sharing feature that provides an easy, fast, and secure way to distribute data. You learned about share objects and considered several basic options for using these features. And we walked through two examples: a simple way to share a table and an advanced way to share one by using a secure view.

CHAPTER 6

Getting Started with Snowpark

Snowpark is a powerful developer framework provided by Snowflake, designed to simplify the process of building and deploying data-driven applications directly within Snowflake's environment.

Snowpark leverages Snowflake's inherent strengths, including automatic scaling, secure data sharing, zero-copy cloning, and Time Travel, to provide a unified and efficient environment for data engineering, data science, and application development. Whether you're transforming data, building complex pipelines, executing machine learning workflows, or embedding business logic, Snowpark equips you with the necessary tools and performance capabilities to excel.

It extends Snowflake's capabilities by allowing developers to write code in their preferred programming languages, such as Python, Java, and Scala, while leveraging Snowflake's scalability and performance.

Key Features of Snowpark

- **Language support**: Snowpark provides native support for several popular programming languages.
  - Python is a versatile and widely adopted language, particularly strong in data science and machine learning.

- Java is a robust and enterprise-grade language well-suited for building scalable applications.

- Scala is a functional and object-oriented language often used in big data processing frameworks like Spark.

This multilanguage support empowers developers to choose the language that best fits their expertise and project requirements, providing flexibility and fostering collaboration across teams with diverse skill sets. This chapter works with Snowpark in Python, because it is the most commonly used language.

- **Pushdown optimization**: A key advantage of Snowpark is its ability to push computations directly to the Snowflake engine. Instead of transferring data to a client machine for processing, Snowpark translates the code written in Python, Java, or Scala into SQL-like operations. It executes them within Snowflake's compute resources. This minimizes data movement, reduces latency, and maximizes performance by leveraging Snowflake's highly optimized query engine and scalable infrastructure.

- **Server-side DataFrame API**: Snowpark introduces a DataFrame API that allows developers to work with data in a familiar, object-oriented manner. This API offers a rich set of operations for manipulating data, including filtering, aggregation, joining, and transformation. The DataFrame API simplifies the development of complex data workflows by providing a consistent and intuitive interface, making it easier to read, write, and maintain code.

- **User-defined functions and stored procedures**: Snowpark enhances extensibility through UDFs and stored procedures. Developers can define custom business logic using UDFs to execute scalar operations on individual data rows, while stored procedures allow encapsulating and executing complex workflows within Snowflake.

- **Seamless integration with Snowflake features**: Snowpark fully integrates with Snowflake's security, data governance, and data sharing features, providing a consistent and secure environment.

This seamless integration streamlines data access control, ensures compliance, and simplifies data sharing with internal and external stakeholders.

Setting up Snowpark

To get started with Snowpark in Python, you need to open an integrated development environment (IDE) on your local machine and create a new virtual Python environment (or use an existing one). You need a Python version of 3.8 or later.

Install Snowpark using the following command.

```
pip install snowflake-snowpark-python
```

Run the following to check if Snowpark is installed correctly.

```
pip show snowflake-snowpark-python
```

You see something similar to the screenshot shown in Figure 6-1.

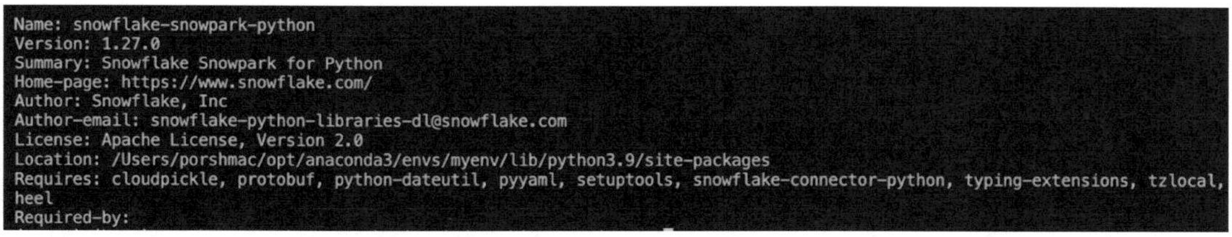

```
Name: snowflake-snowpark-python
Version: 1.27.0
Summary: Snowflake Snowpark for Python
Home-page: https://www.snowflake.com/
Author: Snowflake, Inc
Author-email: snowflake-python-libraries-dl@snowflake.com
License: Apache License, Version 2.0
Location: /Users/porshmac/opt/anaconda3/envs/myenv/lib/python3.9/site-packages
Requires: cloudpickle, protobuf, python-dateutil, pyyaml, setuptools, snowflake-connector-python, typing-extensions, tzlocal,
heel
Required-by:
```

Figure 6-1. *Verify Snowpark installation*

In Snowflake, create a new database and schema (or use an existing one) using the worksheet.

```
create database snowpark_ch7;
create schema output;
```

Next, let's go over authenticating and connecting to Snowflake.

CHAPTER 6 GETTING STARTED WITH SNOWPARK

In your IDE, create a new Python file: ch7_snowpark.py. Then, paste the following code to authenticate and connect to Snowflake.

```python
from snowflake.snowpark import Session

def initiateSession():
    connection_parameters = {
        "account": <account_name>,
        "user": <username>,
        "password": <password>,
        "role": "Accountadmin",
        "warehouse": "compute_wh",
        "database": "snowpark_ch7",
        "schema": "output"
    }
    session = Session.builder.configs(connection_parameters).create()
    return session

session = initiateSession()
print(session.sql("SELECT current_version()").collect())
# Verify connection
```

In this Python function, you can get account_name from Admin ➤ Accounts ➤ Manage URLs. It is the first part of the URL in the Current URL field, before .snowflakecomputing.com. It's highlighted in Figure 6-2.

CHAPTER 6   GETTING STARTED WITH SNOWPARK

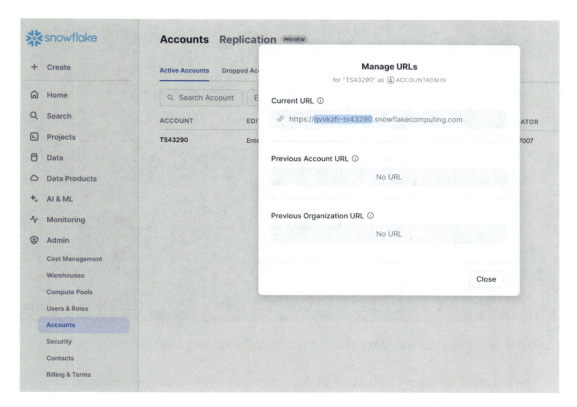

Figure 6-2. *Get account_name from URL*

You may use the username and password you usually use to log in to your Snowflake account.

Make sure to use the correct database name and schema name. Use this schema to save the transformed data to a table later.

Now, you can save your Python file and run it using your IDE (see Figure 6-3).

Chapter 6 Getting Started with Snowpark

Figure 6-3. Initiate Snowpark session and verify connection

The current_version() function in this code returns the current version of Snowflake. In the example shown in Figure 6-2, '9.2.7' refers to the Snowflake database version.

Snowpark DataFrame Operations

Snowpark DataFrame operations provide powerful ways to manipulate and analyze data.

The following command creates a DataFrame based on customer table data. The show command displays the output of the DataFrame (see Figure 6-4).

```
df = session.table("SNOWFLAKE_SAMPLE_DATA.TPCH_SF1.CUSTOMER")
df.show()
```

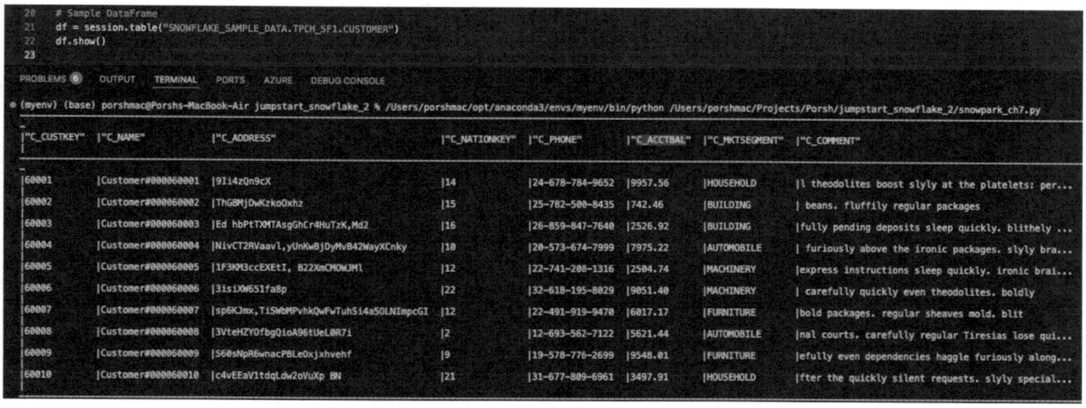

CHAPTER 6 GETTING STARTED WITH SNOWPARK

Figure 6-4. Displaying a sample DataFrame

Now let's make some transformations to the DataFrame and display the outputs to see the results.

Snowpark DataFrames allow developers to perform SQL-like operations programmatically. The following are some common operations.

- **Filtering** allows you to select rows based on specific criteria; for example, filtering data for account balances greater than 5000 and less than 10000.

  ```
  filtered_df = df.filter((df["C_ACCTBAL"] > 5000) & (df["C_ACCTBAL"] < 10000))
  ```

- **Aggregation** enables you to perform calculations on groups of rows; for example, aggregating by nation key and computing the average account balance.

  ```
  aggregated_df = df.group_by("C_NATIONKEY").agg({"C_ACCTBAL": "avg"})
  ```

- **Ordering** allows you to sort rows based on one or more columns; for example, ordering data by account balance in descending order

  ```
  ordered_df = df.sort("C_ACCTBAL", ascending=False)
  ```

- **Joining tables** combines data from multiple tables based on a related column; for example, joining customer and orders tables on customer key.

  ```
  orders_df = session.table("SNOWFLAKE_SAMPLE_DATA.TPCH_SF1.ORDERS")
  joined_df = df.join(orders_df, df["C_CUSTKEY"] == orders_df["O_CUSTKEY"])
  ```

CHAPTER 6   GETTING STARTED WITH SNOWPARK

- **Window functions** allow you to perform calculations across a set of rows related to the current row.

The following example illustrates calculating the running total (see Figure 6-5).

```
from snowflake.snowpark.window import Window
from snowflake.snowpark.functions import sum, col
window = Window.order_by(col("O_ORDERDATE"))
orders_df = session.table("SNOWFLAKE_SAMPLE_DATA.TPCH_SF1.ORDERS")
running_total_df = orders_df.with_column("running_total", sum(col("O_TOTALPRICE")).over(window))
running_total_df.show()
```

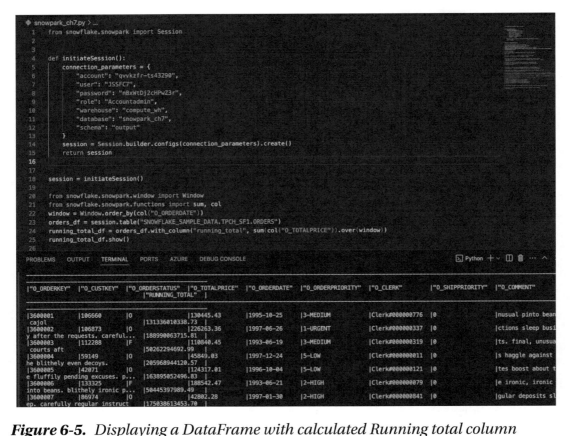

Figure 6-5. Displaying a DataFrame with calculated Running total column

108

You can **write a DataFrame** to a Snowflake database table using the following Snowpark command.

```
running_total_df.write.mode("overwrite").save_as_table("orders_running_total")
```

User-Defined Functions

Snowpark allows you to write custom user-defined functions (UDFs) in Python, Java, or Scala.

To create a Python UDF, register it in Snowflake and use it in a SQL query.

```python
# Define a Python function to calculate discount
def calculate_discount(price, discount):
    return price * (1 - discount / 100)

# Register the UDF with Snowflake
from snowflake.snowpark.types import FloatType
session.udf.register(
    func=calculate_discount,
    name="calculate_discount_udf",
    input_types=[FloatType(), FloatType()],
    return_type=FloatType()
)

# Use the UDF in a SQL query
result_df = session.sql(
    """
    SELECT O_CUSTKEY,
    calculate_discount_udf(O_TOTALPRICE, 10) AS discounted_price
    FROM SNOWFLAKE_SAMPLE_DATA.TPCH_SF1.ORDERS
    """
)
result_df.show()
```

CHAPTER 6 GETTING STARTED WITH SNOWPARK

Figure 6-6 is a screenshot example.

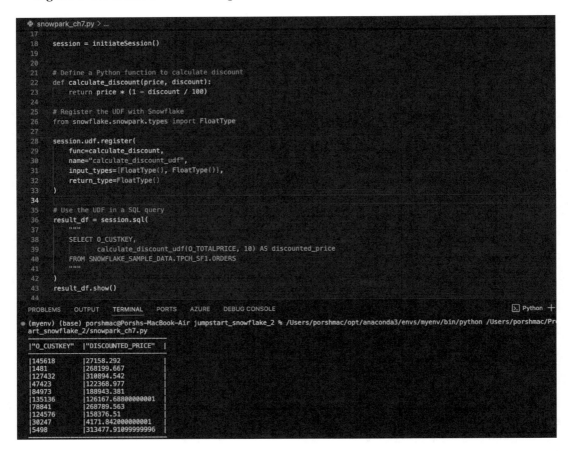

Figure 6-6. *Displaying a DataFrame with a column calculated by created UDF*

Stored Procedures

Snowpark stored procedures enable you to encapsulate complex logic into reusable units that can be executed as a single unit.

The following is an example of copying data from one table to another.

```
from snowflake.snowpark.types import StringType

def copy_data(session: Session, source_table: str, target_table: str) -> str:
    source_df = session.table(source_table)
    source_df.write.save_as_table(target_table, mode="overwrite")
```

CHAPTER 6 GETTING STARTED WITH SNOWPARK

```
    return f"Data successfully copied from {source_table} to
    {target_table}"

session.sproc.register(
    func=copy_data,
    name="copy_data_sproc",
    input_types=[StringType(), StringType()],
    return_type=StringType(),
    packages=["snowflake-snowpark-python"]
)
#Calling the stored procedure
result = session.call("copy_data_sproc", "MY_DATABASE.MY_SCHEMA.SOURCE_TABLE", "MY_DATABASE.MY_SCHEMA.TARGET_TABLE")
print(result)
```

Figure 6-7 is a screenshot example.

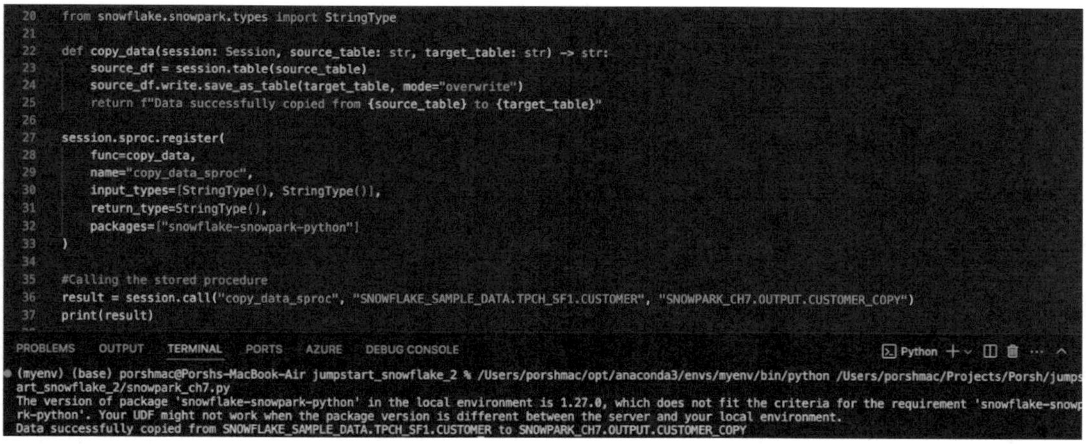

Figure 6-7. Executing stored procedure to copy data from one table to another

Now, you can verify that the stored procedure is executed successfully by checking a new copied table in the output schema.

CHAPTER 6 GETTING STARTED WITH SNOWPARK

Machine Learning Integration with Snowpark

Snowpark empowers you to integrate machine learning models directly into your Snowflake environment. You can leverage libraries such as scikit-learn to train and deploy machine learning models directly within Snowflake. Let's train and deploy a simple model.

For this use case, you need to install the scikit-learn and pandas libraries. Use the following commands in your terminal.

```
pip install scikit-learn
pip install pandas
```

The following script demonstrates how to train a simple machine learning model using scikit-learn, store it in Snowflake, and deploy it as a UDF for real-time predictions using Snowpark.

```python
from snowflake.snowpark.types import FloatType, StringType
from sklearn.linear_model import LinearRegression
import pandas as pd
import pickle
import base64

# Step 1: Train a simple model
X = pd.DataFrame([1, 2, 3, 4, 5])
y = pd.DataFrame([2, 4, 5, 4, 5])
model = LinearRegression()
model.fit(X, y)
```

Create a simple linear regression model. The model is trained on five data points, where X represents input values, and y represents the target.

```python
# Step 2: Serialize the model (Base64 encoding)
model_bytes = pickle.dumps(model)
model_base64 = base64.b64encode(model_bytes).decode("utf-8")
# Convert to Base64 string
```

Use `pickle` to serialize the trained model into a binary format. The binary data is then encoded into Base64 to ensure it can be stored as text in Snowflake.

```
# Step 3: Create a table to store the model (if not exists)
session.sql("CREATE TABLE IF NOT EXISTS model_storage (model VARIANT)").
collect()
```

Create a Snowflake table named model_storage with a VARIANT column to store the model. The VARIANT type is used because it supports JSON-like structures, allowing you to store Base64-encoded text.

```
# Step 4: Store the model in Snowflake
session.sql(f"INSERT INTO model_storage SELECT PARSE_JSON('\"{model_base64}\"')").collect()
print("c Model successfully stored in Snowflake!")
```

Insert the Base64-encoded model into the Snowflake table. The PARSE_JSON function ensures the value is stored as a valid JSON string.

You can verify that the model is saved in the model_storage table in Snowflake, as shown in Figure 6-8.

Figure 6-8. *Displaying the model_storage table created by Snowpark*

```
# Step 5: Define a UDF for model prediction
def predict(model_base64, input_value):
    model_bytes = base64.b64decode(model_base64)
    model = pickle.loads(model_bytes)
    return model.predict([[input_value]])[0][0]
```

```
session.udf.register(
    func=predict,
    name="predict_linear",
    return_type=FloatType(),
    input_types=[StringType(), FloatType()],
    packages=["scikit-learn", "pandas", "numpy"],
    replace=True
)
print("✓ UDF 'predict_linear' registered successfully!")
```

Define a UDF that decodes the Base64 model, deserializes it into a usable Python object, and runs predictions on new input data.

The UDF is registered in Snowflake, allowing users to call predict_linear() directly in SQL queries.

```
# Step 6: Retrieve and deserialize the model from Snowflake
stored_model_base64 = session.sql("SELECT model::STRING FROM model_storage").collect()[0][0]
stored_model_bytes = base64.b64decode(stored_model_base64)
loaded_model = pickle.loads(stored_model_bytes)
```

Fetch the Base64-encoded model from Snowflake. The model is decoded and deserialized back into a usable Python object.

```
# Step 7: Test the retrieved model
test_input = 6
predicted_output = loaded_model.predict([[test_input]])[0][0]
print(f"✓ Prediction for input {test_input}: {predicted_output}")
```

Provide a new input value (6) and use the retrieved model to make a prediction. The predicted output is displayed.

The output with prediction is shown in Figure 6-9.

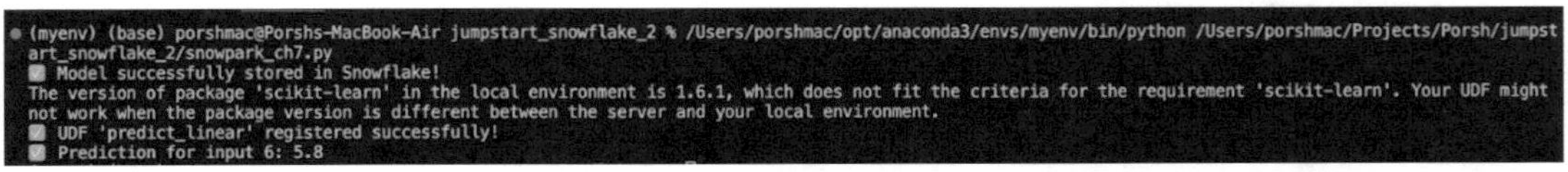

Figure 6-9. Displaying the linear model prediction for imputed test value

This approach allows you to deploy ML models directly in Snowflake, making them available for real-time analytics and SQL-based predictions.

Summary

Snowpark provides numerous benefits to organizations using Snowflake.

- **Unified environment**: Snowpark eliminates the need for ETL tools and enables direct computation within Snowflake.

- **Scalability**: Processes are executed on Snowflake's cloud infrastructure, ensuring scalability and reliability.

- **Ease of use**: Familiar programming paradigms and language support make it accessible to developers.

- **Cost efficiency**: Reduces data movement and enables cost-effective compute usage.

Snowpark offers a transformative approach to building data-driven applications within Snowflake. By extending Snowflake's capabilities with support for popular programming languages, Snowpark empowers developers to leverage their existing skills and preferred programming paradigms. Whether you are performing data transformations, implementing machine learning workflows, or building end-to-end data pipelines, Snowpark provides the tools and performance capabilities needed to succeed.

CHAPTER 7

Snowflake with Apache Iceberg

Apache Iceberg is a popular open source table format. It has a large community and support from top vendors. The adoption of the Iceberg format is increasing every year. Snowflake also introduced integration with the Apache Iceberg format, which allows managed Iceberg catalog or integration with an external Iceberg catalog. In this chapter, you learn more about integration with Apache Iceberg and Snowflake.

Apache Iceberg allows you to build a lake house solution. You need to bring our computing and storage, and this would be enough to create a stand-alone analytics solution.

When thinking about the collaboration between Snowflake and Iceberg, we should rely on existing use cases that are supported by Snowflake as well as overall areas for using Iceberg with Snowflake.

In a typical implementation, Snowflake is used as a data warehouse with storage and computing capabilities like any other traditional data warehouse.

There are some cases when the use of Apache Iceberg might help as a complementary tool.

- The size of a Snowflake implementation could be massive. It would be expensive to process the data using Snowflake, and using external computing could drop the cost of Snowflake.

- Some workloads require querying massive raw data. This data could be stored in separate storage and registered in the Iceberg catalog.

CHAPTER 7　SNOWFLAKE WITH APACHE ICEBERG

- Big organizations might have multiple data solutions, including Snowflake, Databricks, and other SQL engines. Iceberg might serve as a standard format that connects data and allows the creation of your own computing.

In other words, we mostly talk about the Iceberg in the context of convenience and cost optimization. We don't compare speed and performance against Snowflake.

Data Platform Architecture

Before exploring Iceberg and Snowflake integration, let's examine the typical data platform architecture. Figure 7-1 highlights the key components of a data platform.

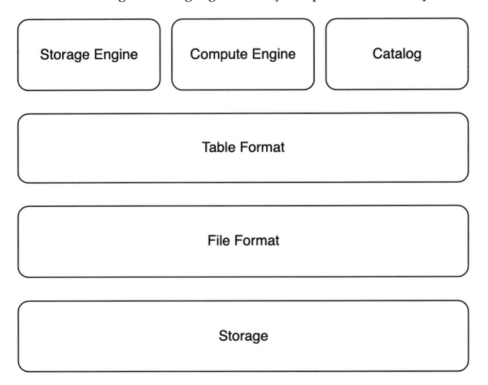

Figure 7-1. *Data platform components*

Table 7-1 describes each element of the architecture.

Table 7-1. Key Elements of a Data Platform

Element	Description
File Format	A file format of data such as CSV, JSON, Parquet, and so on
Table Format	An abstraction layer over file formats, such as Hive, Iceberg, or Delta
Catalog	Stores metadata about data such as location, statistics, and so on
Compute Engine	Compute power that executes queries, reads, processes, and writes data
Storage Engine	Helps manage underlying data
Storage	A place for storing the data, such as cloud storage like AWS S3, GCP Storage, Azure Storage, HDFS, NAS, or DAS

There are many data platform vendors on the market, and they offer different variations of components, starting from tightly coupled and closed systems to opened systems.

You might guess where Snowflake fit. It depends on the configuration. By default, it feels tightly coupled and close, even knowing that it decoupled storage and compute. The more components used, such as external tables, the more open it becomes.

Table format is crucial in the Lakehouse approach. The table format answers the question about what data is in the table. Assume we have an AWS S3 bucket with a folder. The folder contains lots of data files in JSON. JSON is a file format, and it would be hard to query this data. Table format provides the option to leverage metadata, including the schema of the table, and we can write queries against this data using SQL.

Getting Started with Apache Iceberg

Apache Iceberg is an open source table format for high-performance analytics. It adds a table for compute engines like Spark, Trino, and Athena. The Iceberg table works and feels like an SQL table.

It has many benefits for data engineers and analytics workloads.

- schema evolution
- hidden partitions

- partition evolution
- time travel

Snowflake has similar features, but they are hidden under the hood. Apache Iceberg contains multiple key layers.

- The catalog has a reference to the current metadata file.
- Metadata contains three file types.
  - Metadata files contain information about tables such as schema, partitions, snapshots, location, and so on.
  - Manifest files have metadata about files by collecting and storing information about data, such as statistics or row count.
  - Manifest lists contain manifest files per snapshot.
- Data is the actual storage layer where data is stored.

Later in the chapter, we create an Iceberg table and explore files.

The Role of a Catalog

The primary goal of a catalog is to answer the question of where to find data. The table format tells you what is stored in the data.

Note According to Apache Iceberg documentation, "Catalogs manage a collection of tables that are usually grouped into namespaces. The most important responsibility of a catalog is tracking a table's current metadata, which is provided by the catalog when you load a table."

There are several options for Iceberg catalog implementations.

- REST API
- The Hive Metastore is tracked metadata.
- JDBC tracks metadata in the external relation database.

- Nessie tracks metadata with git-like version control.

- AWS Glue catalog is a managed Hive Metastore. It tracks metadata across AWS services, such as Athena, Glue, and Redshift Spectrum.

There are more catalogs existing on the market. Their primary goal remains the same—track metadata about the data and server as an entry point for working with data by different data tools.

Snowflake and Iceberg Integrations

Snowflake announced integration with the Apache Polaris catalog.

Apache Polaris is an open source, fully featured catalog for Apache Iceberg. It implements Iceberg's REST API, enabling seamless multi-engine interoperability across a wide range of platforms, including Apache Doris, Apache Flink, Apache Spark, StarRocks, and Trino. It allows the management of Iceberg tables and metadata.

It supports two options.

- Managed Iceberg catalog by Snowflake

- Use an external Iceberg catalog

Table 7-2 summarizes available options and highlights who is responsible for various elements of a data platform architecture.

Table 7-2. Data Platform Available Options

Options	Storage Engine	Compute Engine	Catalog	Table Format	File Format	Storage
Snowflake as is	Snowflake	Snowflake	Snowflake	Snowflake	CSV, JSON, ORC, Parquet, XML	AWS S3, Azure Blob Storage, GCP Storage
Snowflake with Apache Iceberg	Snowflake	Snowflake, Trino, Flink, Spark, DuckDB, PyArrow	Snowflake, Polaris, Glue	Iceberg		

Snowflake with Apache Iceberg allows you to start using data in Apache Iceberg format stored in external storage accounts without ingesting it into Snowflake.

Before the Iceberg integration, Snowflake allowed you to use external tables and query data with Snowflake compute. With the Polaris catalog, you can still use the external tables feature, but this allows you to query Apache Iceberg data. In addition, there is another option: use your own compute to query Iceberg tables.

This chapter reviews examples of the Snowflake-managed Iceberg catalog. In Snowflake documentation, you can review the example of using the external Iceberg catalog.

Creating Snowflake Iceberg Table

Let's create an Iceberg table using Python and Jupyter Notebook. We use Conda.

Follow the guide at https://docs.anaconda.com/miniconda/install/#quick-command-line-install to install your operating system.

In the IDE of your choice, you need to create a new folder or project and add the environment.yml file.

Inside the file, specify all the dependencies.

```
name: iceberg-lab
channels:
  - conda-forge
dependencies:
  - findspark=2.0.1
  - jupyter=1.0.0
  - pyspark=3.5.0
  - openjdk=11.0.13
```

You need to disable SSL.

```
conda config --set ssl_verify no
```

Then, create a virtual environment using Conda.

```
conda env create -f environment.yml
```

And activate the environment.

```
conda activate iceberg-lab
```

Next, open SnowSight and create the required objects for our exercise.

```
CREATE WAREHOUSE iceberg_lab;
CREATE ROLE iceberg_lab;
CREATE DATABASE iceberg_lab;
CREATE SCHEMA iceberg_lab;
GRANT ALL ON DATABASE iceberg_lab TO ROLE iceberg_lab WITH GRANT OPTION;
GRANT ALL ON SCHEMA iceberg_lab.iceberg_lab TO ROLE iceberg_lab WITH GRANT OPTION;;
GRANT ALL ON WAREHOUSE iceberg_lab TO ROLE iceberg_lab WITH GRANT OPTION;;

CREATE USER iceberg_lab
    PASSWORD='Iceberglab2024!',
    LOGIN_NAME='ICEBERG_LAB',
    MUST_CHANGE_PASSWORD=FALSE,
    DISABLED=FALSE,
    DEFAULT_WAREHOUSE='ICEBERG_LAB',
    DEFAULT_NAMESPACE='ICEBERG_LAB.ICEBERG_LAB',
    DEFAULT_ROLE='ICEBERG_LAB';

GRANT ROLE iceberg_lab TO USER iceberg_lab;
GRANT ROLE iceberg_lab TO ROLE accountadmin;
GRANT ROLE accountadmin TO USER iceberg_lab;
```

In this case, we use AWS, and the external volume depends on AWS S3. Snowflake has a guide on external volumes at https://docs.snowflake.com/en/user-guide/tables-iceberg-configure-external-volume-s3.

In the AWS console, create a new S3 bucket jumpstart-iceberg-snowflake. The bucket serves as an external storage for your data in Iceberg file format.

You should create a new policy in AWS Identity and Access Management (IAM): jumpstart-iceberg-policy. Figure 7-2 shows the AWS console policy permissions.

CHAPTER 7 SNOWFLAKE WITH APACHE ICEBERG

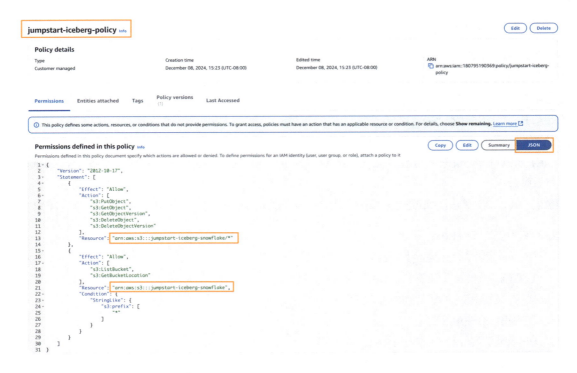

Figure 7-2. *AWS IAM policy*

```
{
    "Version": "2012-10-17",
    "Statement": [
        {
            "Effect": "Allow",
            "Action": [
                "s3:PutObject",
                "s3:GetObject",
                "s3:GetObjectVersion",
                "s3:DeleteObject",
                "s3:DeleteObjectVersion"
            ],
            "Resource": "arn:aws:s3:::jumpstart-iceberg-snowflake/*"
        },
        {
            "Effect": "Allow",
            "Action": [
```

CHAPTER 7 SNOWFLAKE WITH APACHE ICEBERG

```
                "s3:ListBucket",
                "s3:GetBucketLocation"
            ],
            "Resource": "arn:aws:s3:::jumpstart-iceberg-snowflake",
            "Condition": {
                "StringLike": {
                    "s3:prefix": [
                        "*"
                    ]
                }
            }
        }
    ]
}
```

Next, add a new role in AWS IAM: `jumpstart-iceberg-role`. This role should have `jumpstart-iceberg-policy.` Figure 7-3 shows the IAM role menu in the AWS console.

Figure 7-3. *AWS IAM role*

Copy the ARN from the role in the following format.

`'arn:aws:iam::<YOUR ACCOUNT NUMBER>:role/jumpstart-iceberg-role'`

The ARN is needed to establish a connection between the Snowflake AWS account and our AWS account, where we created the bucket.

125

CHAPTER 7 SNOWFLAKE WITH APACHE ICEBERG

In SnowSight, you can create an external volume now.

```
USE ROLE accountadmin;

CREATE OR REPLACE EXTERNAL VOLUME iceberg_lab_vol
   STORAGE_LOCATIONS =
      (
         (
            NAME = 'iceberg-lab'
            STORAGE_PROVIDER = 'S3'
            STORAGE_BASE_URL = 's3://jumpstart-iceberg-snowflake'
            STORAGE_AWS_ROLE_ARN = 'arn:aws:iam::<YOUR ACCOUNT NUMBER:role/
            jumpstart-iceberg-role'
            STORAGE_AWS_EXTERNAL_ID = 'iceberg_table_external_id'
         )
      );

GRANT ALL ON EXTERNAL VOLUME iceberg_lab_vol TO ROLE iceberg_lab WITH
GRANT OPTION;
```

Next, grant Snowflake's IAM user permissions to access the S3 bucket in our AWS account using the AWS trust policy.

To find Snowflake's IAM role, run the following command.

```
DESC EXTERNAL VOLUME iceberg_lab_vol;
```

It looks similar to the "STORAGE_AWS_IAM_USER_ARN":"arn:aws:iam::881490105466:user/a98t0000-s" example.

In the AWS account, open jumpstart-iceberg-role and select the **Trust relationships** tab. Figure 7-4 shows a menu of trust relationships between our account and the Snowflake account.

CHAPTER 7　SNOWFLAKE WITH APACHE ICEBERG

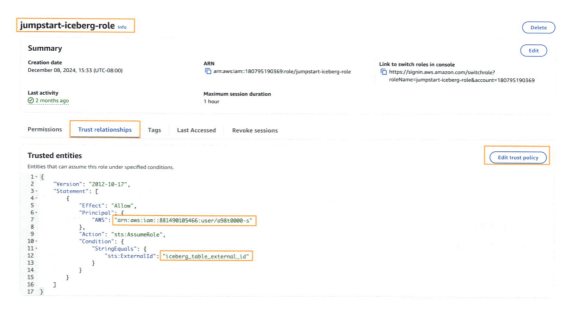

Figure 7-4. Trust relationships

You should use your ARN and make sure the external ID matches your name.

Finally, create the Iceberg table in Snowflake. Open SnowSight and run the following SQL to create a table.

```
USE ROLE iceberg_lab;
USE DATABASE iceberg_lab;
USE SCHEMA iceberg_lab;
CREATE OR REPLACE ICEBERG TABLE customer_iceberg (
    c_custkey INTEGER,
    c_name STRING,
    c_address STRING,
    c_nationkey INTEGER,
    c_phone STRING,
    c_acctbal INTEGER,
    c_mktsegment STRING,
    c_comment STRING
)
    CATALOG='SNOWFLAKE'
    EXTERNAL_VOLUME='iceberg_lab_vol'
    BASE_LOCATION='';
```

CHAPTER 7 SNOWFLAKE WITH APACHE ICEBERG

This example uses a Snowflake-managed catalog.

Next, ingest data using available sample data.

```
INSERT INTO customer_iceberg
  SELECT * FROM snowflake_sample_data.tpch_sf1.customer;
```

The query inserts 150,000 rows into Iceberg format.

Use the Snowflake compute warehouse to query the data.

```
SELECT
    *
FROM customer_iceberg c
INNER JOIN snowflake_sample_data.tpch_sf1.nation n
    ON c.c_nationkey = n.n_nationkey;
```

Snowflake has written data into an external volume (S3 bucket) where we can review the data and metadata. Figure 7-5 shows metadata files for our table in a Snowflake-managed catalog.

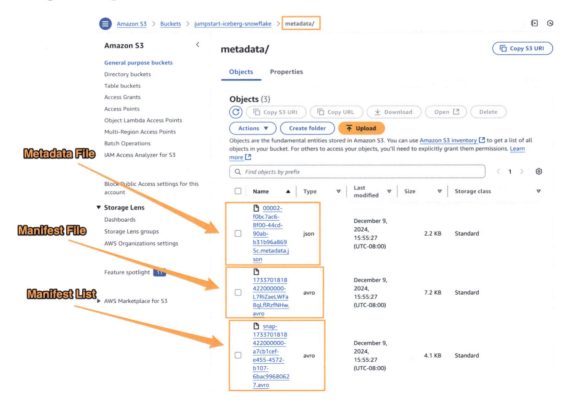

Figure 7-5. Iceberg metadata files in S3

CHAPTER 7 SNOWFLAKE WITH APACHE ICEBERG

Figure 7-6 shows actual data files in Parquet file format.

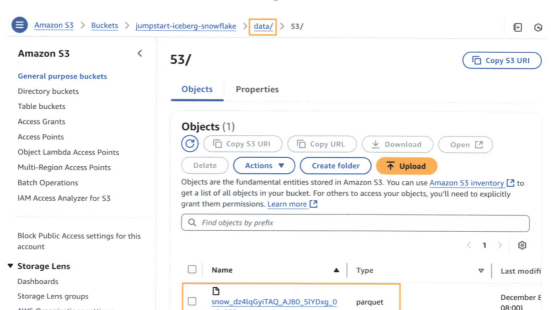

Figure 7-6. *Iceberg data files in S3*

It is important to know that you can't just read Iceberg files. Iceberg requires you to have the catalog.

Query Iceberg Table with External Compute

Querying data in a Snowflake warehouse is simple. The biggest advantage of using Iceberg data is to replace external tables in Snowflake. It is proven that Iceberg tables are faster than traditional external tables with simple Parquet or JSON file format. However, it does not bring any cost savings. The true cost savings might happen if we bring external computing, such as Apache Spark, Trino, DuckDB, and ClickHouse.

Let's review the example of using Apache Spark for querying our Snowflake Iceberg table.

Using the same Conda environment, you can launch Jupyter Notebook with Apache Spark.

The code is available in the code repo for this chapter. The notebook contains all commands, and you should complete the following parameters.

- Snowflake catalog URI
- Snowflake role
- Snowflake username and password
- AWS region
- AWS access and secret key

```
import os
os.environ['SPARK_HOME'] = '~/anaconda3/envs/iceberg-lab/lib/python3.12/site-packages/pyspark'
import findspark
findspark.init()
findspark.find()

os.environ['SNOWFLAKE_CATALOG_URI'] = "jdbc:snowflake://gj91678.eu-central-1.snowflakecomputing.com"
os.environ['SNOWFLAKE_ROLE'] = "ICEBERG_LAB"
os.environ['SNOWFLAKE_USERNAME'] = "ICEBERG_LAB"
os.environ['SNOWFLAKE_PASSWORD'] = "password"
# Environment variables for AWS
os.environ['PACKAGES'] = "org.apache.iceberg:iceberg-spark-runtime-3.5_2.12:1.4.1,net.snowflake:snowflake-jdbc:3.14.2,software.amazon.awssdk:bundle:2.20.160,software.amazon.awssdk:url-connection-client:2.20.160"
os.environ['AWS_REGION'] = "eu-central-1"
os.environ['AWS_ACCESS_KEY_ID'] = "AKIASUGB3VRQ2VETAWJZ"
os.environ['AWS_SECRET_ACCESS_KEY'] = "secret"
```

Start a Spark session.

```
import pyspark
from pyspark.sql import SparkSession

spark = SparkSession.builder.appName('iceberg_lab')\
    .config('spark.jars.packages', os.environ['PACKAGES'])\
```

```
    .config('spark.sql.extensions', 'org.apache.iceberg.spark.extensions.
      IcebergSparkSessionExtensions')\
    .config("spark.driver.allowMultipleContexts","true")\
    .getOrCreate()
```

Snowflake provided a list of environment variables to connect to a catalog. This example connects AWS. However, there are options for Microsoft Azure and Google Cloud.

```
spark.conf.set("spark.sql.defaultCatalog", "snowflake_catalog")
spark.conf.set("spark.sql.catalog.snowflake_catalog", "org.apache.iceberg.
spark.SparkCatalog")
spark.conf.set("spark.sql.catalog.snowflake_catalog.catalog-impl", "org.
apache.iceberg.snowflake.SnowflakeCatalog")
spark.conf.set("spark.sql.catalog.snowflake_catalog.uri",
os.environ['SNOWFLAKE_CATALOG_URI'])
spark.conf.set("spark.sql.catalog.snowflake_catalog.jdbc.role",
os.environ['SNOWFLAKE_ROLE'])
spark.conf.set("spark.sql.catalog.snowflake_catalog.jdbc.user",
os.environ['SNOWFLAKE_USERNAME'])
spark.conf.set("spark.sql.catalog.snowflake_catalog.jdbc.password",
os.environ['SNOWFLAKE_PASSWORD'])
spark.conf.set("spark.sql.iceberg.vectorization.enabled", "false")
# aws
spark.conf.set("spark.sql.catalog.snowflake_catalog.io-impl", "org.apache.
iceberg.aws.s3.S3FileIO")
spark.conf.set("spark.hadoop.fs.s3a.impl", "org.apache.hadoop.fs.s3a.
S3AFileSystem")
spark.conf.set("spark.hadoop.fs.s3a.aws.credentials.provider", "org.apache.
hadoop.fs.s3a.SimpleAWSCredentialsProvider")
spark.conf.set("spark.hadoop.fs.s3a.access.key", os.environ['AWS_ACCESS_
KEY_ID'])
spark.conf.set("spark.hadoop.fs.s3a.secret.key", os.environ['AWS_SECRET_
ACCESS_KEY'])
spark.conf.set("spark.hadoop.fs.s3a.endpoint", "s3.amazonaws.com")
spark.conf.set("spark.hadoop.fs.s3a.endpoint.region", os.environ['AWS_REGION'])
```

CHAPTER 7 SNOWFLAKE WITH APACHE ICEBERG

After connecting to the Snowflake catalog, you can query the data using Spark SQL.

```
spark.sql("SHOW NAMESPACES IN ICEBERG_LAB").show()
spark.sql("USE ICEBERG_LAB.ICEBERG_LAB")
spark.sql("SHOW TABLES").show()
df = spark.table("iceberg_lab.iceberg_lab.customer_iceberg")
df.show()
```

```
+---------+---------------+--------------------+-----------+---------------+---------+------------+--------------------+
|C_CUSTKEY|         C_NAME|           C_ADDRESS|C_NATIONKEY|        C_PHONE|C_ACCTBAL|C_MKTSEGMENT|           C_COMMENT|
+---------+---------------+--------------------+-----------+---------------+---------+------------+--------------------+
|        1|Customer#000000001|    IVhzIApeRb ot,c,E|         15|25-989-741-2988|      712|    BUILDING|to the even, regu...|
|        2|Customer#000000002|XSTf4,NCwDVaWNe6t...|         13|23-768-687-3665|      122|  AUTOMOBILE|l accounts. blith...|
|        3|Customer#000000003|        MG9kdTD2WBHm|          1|11-719-748-3364|     7498|  AUTOMOBILE| deposits eat sly...|
|        4|Customer#000000004|         XxVSJsLAGtn|          4|14-128-190-5944|     2867|   MACHINERY| requests. final,...|
|        5|Customer#000000005|KvpyuHCplrB84WgAi...|          3|13-750-942-6364|      794|   HOUSEHOLD|n accounts will h...|
|        6|Customer#000000006|sKZz0CsnMD7mp4Xd0...|         20|30-114-968-4951|     7639|  AUTOMOBILE|tions. even depos...|
|        7|Customer#000000007|TcGe5gaZNgVePxU5k...|         18|28-190-982-9759|     9562|  AUTOMOBILE|ainst the ironic,...|
|        8|Customer#000000008|I0B10bB0AymmC, 0P...|         17|27-147-574-9335|     6820|    BUILDING|among the slyly r...|
|        9|Customer#000000009|xKiAFTjUsCuxfeleN...|          8|18-338-906-3675|     8324|   FURNITURE|r theodolites acc...|
|       10|Customer#000000010|6LrEaV6KR6PLVcgl2...|          5|15-741-346-9870|     2754|   HOUSEHOLD|es regular deposi...|
|       11|Customer#000000011|PkWS 3HlXqwTuzrKg...|         23|33-464-151-3439|     -273|    BUILDING|ckages. requests ...|
|       12|Customer#000000012|        9PWKuhzT4Zr1Q|         13|23-791-276-1263|     3396|   HOUSEHOLD| to the carefully...|
|       13|Customer#000000013|nsXQu0oVjD7PM659u...|          3|13-761-547-5974|     3857|    BUILDING|ounts sleep caref...|
|       14|Customer#000000014|       KXkletMlL2JQEA|          1|11-845-129-3851|     5266|   FURNITURE|, ironic packages...|
|       15|Customer#000000015|YtWggXo0Ldwdo7b0y...|         23|33-687-542-7601|     2789|   HOUSEHOLD| platelets. regul...|
|       16|Customer#000000016|    cYiaeMLZSMA0Q2 d0W,|         10|20-781-609-3107|     4681|   FURNITURE|kly silent courts...|
|       17|Customer#000000017|    izrh 6jdqtp2eqdtb...|          2|12-970-682-3487|        6|  AUTOMOBILE|packages wake! bl...|
|       18|Customer#000000018|  3txGO AiuFux3zT0Z...|          6|16-155-215-1315|     5494|    BUILDING|s sleep. carefull...|
|       19|Customer#000000019|   uc,3bHIx84H,wdrmL...|         18|28-396-526-5053|     8915|   HOUSEHOLD| nag. furiously c...|
|       20|Customer#000000020|        JrPk8Pqplj4Ne|         22|32-957-234-8742|     7603|   FURNITURE|g alongside of th...|
+---------+---------------+--------------------+-----------+---------------+---------+------------+--------------------+
```

Summary

This chapter reviewed the integration with Apache Iceberg and learned about managing the Iceberg catalog. We created a Snowflake-managed Iceberg catalog and wrote data into S3. We also reviewed data in S3 and used Apache Spark as an external compute.

CHAPTER 8

Getting Started with Streamlit

In today's data-driven world, the ability to transform complex data into actionable insights is paramount. Streamlit emerges as a powerful Python library specifically designed to simplify this process, allowing you to build and share interactive web applications with remarkable ease. Whether you are a data scientist, machine learning engineer, or business analyst, Streamlit empowers you to showcase your work effectively without requiring extensive web development expertise. This chapter provides a comprehensive exploration of Streamlit's capabilities, guiding you through the process of building and deploying interactive data applications. The following Streamlit topics are covered.

- Basics
- Integration with Snowflake
- Creating a basic Streamlit app
- Creating an interactive Streamlit app
- Error handling

This chapter equips you with the knowledge and skills to harness the power of Streamlit, enabling you to transform your data into insightful and impactful interactive web applications.

Streamlit Basics

Streamlit is an open source Python library that facilitates the rapid creation of interactive web applications for data science and machine learning projects. Its intuitive API and straightforward design philosophy allow developers to focus on their core expertise, which is extracting insights from data, rather than grappling with the complexities of web development.

There are many use cases for using Streamlit with Snowflake, and many times, it just to easily automate data tasks, such as data exploration and visualization, self-service custom solutions, dynamic reporting, and more. By combining the power of Snowflake's data platform with Streamlit's ease of use, you can create a wide range of powerful and interactive data applications.

Key Features of Streamlit

- **Simple and intuitive**: Streamlit's minimalist syntax and declarative approach make it incredibly easy to learn and use, even for those without prior web development experience.

- **Rapid prototyping**: Streamlit's "write and see" development model enables you to iterate quickly on your ideas and see changes reflected in real time, accelerating your development workflow.

- **Interactive widgets**: Streamlit provides a rich set of built-in interactive widgets, such as sliders, buttons, and dropdowns, empowering you to create engaging and dynamic user interfaces.

- **Seamless integration**: Streamlit seamlessly integrates with popular Python data science libraries, including Pandas, NumPy, Scikit-learn, and TensorFlow, allowing you to leverage your existing code and tools.

- **Easy deployment**: Streamlit offers hassle-free deployment options, making it straightforward to share your applications with colleagues, clients, or the wider world.

Integration with Snowflake

Even though you have the option of using Streamlit through its open source Python package, Snowflake makes it super easy to work with Streamlit as it comes included in the Snowflake UI. Instead of moving data and application code outside of the Snowflake environment, developers can use Streamlit to build applications that work directly with data within Snowflake. This integration offers several benefits.

- **Simplified infrastructure management**: Snowflake handles the underlying compute and storage needs for Streamlit applications, removing the overhead of managing external systems.

- **Secure data access**: Streamlit applications leverage Snowflake's role-based access control to manage user access, ensuring data security.

- **Seamless workflow**: Streamlit applications run on Snowflake warehouses and use internal stages for file and data storage, allowing efficient data processing.

- **Integration with Snowflake features**: Streamlit works seamlessly with other Snowflake features like Snowpark, user-defined functions, stored procedures, and the Snowflake Native App Framework.

- **Rapid development**: When using Snowsight, developers benefit from a side-by-side editor and application preview, enabling real-time code adjustments and immediate visualization of changes.

This tight integration allows rapid prototyping and deployment of interactive data applications directly within the Snowflake environment. However, it's important to be mindful of resource consumption, which directly impacts billing. Please be mindful that running a Streamlit app, as well as executing any SQL queries within the app, requires a virtual warehouse. This means that the chosen warehouse remains active as long as the app's WebSocket connection is active, which is approximately 15 minutes after the last use.

> **Tip** To control costs, developers can suspend the virtual warehouse or simply close the web page running the app, allowing the warehouse to auto-suspend.

CHAPTER 8 GETTING STARTED WITH STREAMLIT

Creating a Basic Streamlit App

Let's create a basic Streamlit app that displays the contents of a Snowflake table. The following exercise grants the needed permissions and runs Python code to output the contents of a table.

DISPLAY THE CONTENTS OF A SNOWFLAKE TABLE IN STREAMLIT

Before starting this exercise, make sure you have the appropriate setup and permissions. First, set up a separate database specifically for Streamlit apps.

1. Create a new worksheet or log in through SnowSQL to run the following DDL.

   ```
   CREATE DATABASE STREAMLIT_APPS;
   GRANT USAGE ON DATABASE STREAMLIT_APPS TO ROLE PUBLIC;
   GRANT USAGE ON SCHEMA STREAMLIT_APPS.PUBLIC TO ROLE PUBLIC;
   GRANT CREATE STREAMLIT ON SCHEMA STREAMLIT_APPS.PUBLIC TO ROLE PUBLIC;
   GRANT CREATE STAGE ON SCHEMA STREAMLIT_APPS.PUBLIC TO ROLE PUBLIC;
   ```

Tip While not technically mandatory, using a separate database (or schema) for your Streamlit applications is a strong best practice for organization, security, resource management, and development lifecycle management. It's highly recommended, especially as your projects grow in complexity or if you have multiple developers working on them.

2. Click **Projects + Streamlit**. Click **+Streamlit App**, located on the upper right side of the screen. Fill in the values similar to what is in Figure 8-1.

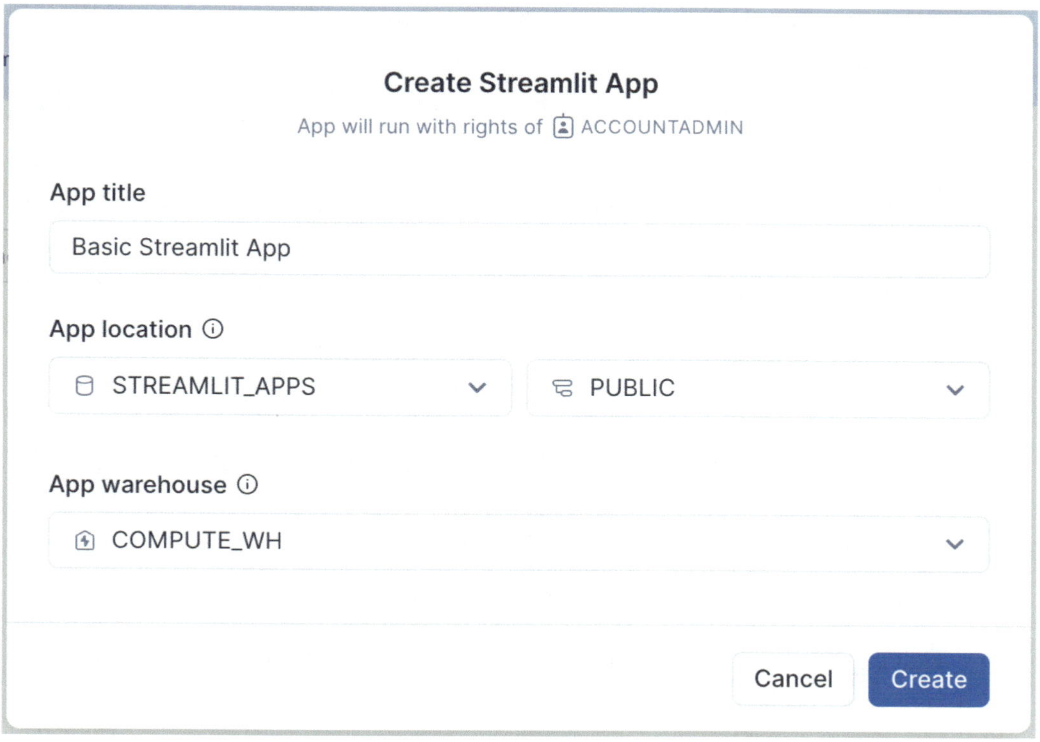

CHAPTER 8 GETTING STARTED WITH STREAMLIT

Figure 8-1. The values in step 1 before clicking Create

3. You'll see your new app load Example Streamlit App. Remove all the Python code from that example and replace it with the following code.

```
# Import python packages
import streamlit as st
import pandas as pd
from snowflake.snowpark.context import get_active_session
```

```
# st.title() Displays the main title of your app. Should be used
sparingly and only once at the top.
st.title("EXERCISE 8.1: DISPLAY THE CONTENTS OF A SNOWFLAKE
TABLE IN STREAMLIT ")
```

```
# Get the Snowflake credentials of the user logged in
session = get_active_session()
```

CHAPTER 8 GETTING STARTED WITH STREAMLIT

```
# Create dataframe from the NATION table, which will be
displayed on the screen
df = session.sql("SELECT * FROM SNOWFLAKE_SAMPLE_DATA.TPCH_SF1.
NATION;").to_pandas()
```

```
# st.header() Displays a header for a section. Good for dividing
your app into logical parts.
st.header("Displaying the NATION table from the Dataframe")
```

```
# Finally, display the contents of the table.
st.dataframe(df)
```

```
st.header("Displaying the NATION table from the Dataframe,
without the row Index")
st.dataframe(df, hide_index=True)
```

4. Click **Run**, located on the upper right side of the page.

Figure 8-2 shows an example of what you see once you complete this exercise. You should see the title, headers, and the data from the showflake_sample_data.tpch.nation table displayed, one with the row index and one without.

Figure 8-2. *What you see once you complete this exercise*

CHAPTER 8   GETTING STARTED WITH STREAMLIT

Creating Interactive Streamlit Apps

Building interactive apps is surprisingly easy with Streamlit in Snowflake. Streamlit's intuitive API and built-in components make it simple to create these interactive elements with Python code. A simple interactive Streamlit dashboard could include data displays, filters, drill-down capability, and more. For example, you could use the st.multiselect component as a way to select one or more options to filter and the st.bar_chart component to display a bar chart of the selected data. These two components are used to build an interactive Streamlit app in the following exercise.

INTERACTIVE STREAMLIT APP

This exercise builds on the work done in the previous exercise and joins the NATION table to the REGION and CUSTOMER tables. This Streamlit app tells you the number of nations and number of customers for each region. This information is displayed in a table and bar chart. In addition, there is an interactive filter that allows you to add or remove both regions and nations, which automatically updates a table and bar chart.

1. Create a new Streamlit app and remove all the example code to start with a blank slate.

2. Add the following code, which includes the needed Python packages, get session credentials, run the Snowflake query to a DataFrame, and give your app a title.

```
# Import python packages
import streamlit as st
import pandas as pd
from snowflake.snowpark.context import get_active_session

# st.title() Displays the main title of your app. Should be used
sparingly and only once at the top.
st.title("EXERCISE 8.2: INTERACTIVE STREAMLIT APP")

# Get the current credentials
session = get_active_session()

query = "select N_NAME as NATION_NAME, R_NAME as REGION_NAME, COUNT(C_CUSTKEY) TOTAL_CUSTOMERS \
COUNT(C_CUSTKEY) TOTAL_CUSTOMERS \
from SNOWFLAKE_SAMPLE_DATA.TPCH_SF1.NATION  \
```

```
    join SNOWFLAKE_SAMPLE_DATA.TPCH_SF1.REGION \
    join SNOWFLAKE_SAMPLE_DATA.TPCH_SF1.CUSTOMER \
    on R_REGIONKEY = N_REGIONKEY AND N_NATIONKEY = C_NATIONKEY \
    GROUP BY 1,2"

    # Create initial dataframe
    df = session.sql(query).to_pandas()
```

3. Add the following code to create an interactive filter menu. The filters include all the available regions and all the available nations.

```
    # Sidebar with filters
    st.sidebar.header('Interactive Filter')
    st.sidebar.divider()
    st.sidebar.subheader('Regions')

    regions = st.sidebar.multiselect(
        "Select one or more regions:",
        options=df["REGION_NAME"].sort_values().unique(),
        default=df["REGION_NAME"].sort_values().unique()
    )

    nations = st.sidebar.multiselect(
        "Select one or more nations:",
        options=df["NATION_NAME"].sort_values().unique(),
        default=df["NATION_NAME"].sort_values().unique()
    )

    # Filter dataframe with selection in
    df_filtered = df.query(
        "REGION_NAME in @regions and \
        NATION_NAME in @nations"
    )
```

4. Add a way for the data to aggregate dynamically when the user removes or adds a region or nation.

```
    # Aggregate the data dynamically
    df_agg = df_filtered.groupby('REGION_NAME').agg(
        TOTAL_NATIONS=('NATION_NAME', 'count'),
```

CHAPTER 8   GETTING STARTED WITH STREAMLIT

```
    , TOTAL_CUSTOMERS=('TOTAL_CUSTOMERS', 'sum')
).reset_index()

st.subheader("Table: Total Nations and Customers per Region")
st.dataframe(df_agg, hide_index=True)

st.subheader("Bar Chart: Total Customers per Region")
st.bar_chart(df_agg.set_index('REGION_NAME')[['TOTAL_
CUSTOMERS']])
```

5. Click **Run** one last time.

Your final product should look something like Figure 8-3. Only the Total Customers per Region data is shown in the bar chart. Try adding an additional bar chart for the Total Nations per Region to this app. Play around with the interactive filters and see how the data changes as you remove or add regions and nations.

Figure 8-3. *The final product of the interactive Streamlit app once you complete this exercise*

141

CHAPTER 8   GETTING STARTED WITH STREAMLIT

Error Handling and Troubleshooting

Now that you know how to build basic apps within Streamlit, it's important to plan for errors and how to handle them. Think of error handling as a way to make your app smart. Instead of crashing or giving confusing messages to the user when something goes wrong, good error handling allows your app to catch those mistakes, show helpful messages, and keep things moving. It makes your app more reliable and user-friendly.

This section walks you through some common errors you might face and how to deal with them, ensuring your app runs smoothly and does not break when things go wrong.

When using Streamlit with Snowflake, you'll likely run into a few types of errors, such as the following.

- **Connection errors** happen when your app can't connect to Snowflake. This could be due to wrong credentials, an issue with the network, or Snowflake being temporarily unavailable.

- **Query errors** occur when your SQL query doesn't run as expected. It might be a typo in the SQL or an invalid table name.

- **Streamlit errors** happen inside Streamlit itself. For example, if the app fails to render a table or plot because of missing data.

Most error handling or help with troubleshooting can be done with a `try-except` block. In Python, it is a mechanism used to handle exceptions or errors that may occur during program execution. How it works is the code within the `try` block is executed normally. However, if an error or exception occurs, the program immediately jumps to the `except` block where the error can be handled or logged. You can also specify more than one type of exception to catch specific errors and take appropriate actions. Using `try-except` helps to create more robust, fault-tolerant applications by handling potential issues instead of letting them disrupt the program flow. Let's take a look at incorporating a `try-except` block in the first exercise's code.

Connection Errors

Figure 8-4 demonstrates how you could add a `try-except` block around the `get_active_session()` function. This would catch any issues related to Snowflake authentication, connection, or session retrieval. When the connection fails, an error is displayed using `st.error()`. `st.stop()` is used to prevent the rest of the code from running, ensuring that we don't try to execute queries without a valid connection.

CHAPTER 8 GETTING STARTED WITH STREAMLIT

```
try:
    session = get_active_session()
    st.success("Successfully connected to Snowflake!")

except Exception as e:
    # If there is an issue with the connection, display the error
    st.error(f"Connection Error: {str(e)}")
    st.stop()  # Prevent further execution if connection fails
```

Figure 8-4. *Wrapping a try-except block around our Snowflake connection*

Query Errors

You can also wrap the query that fetches the data in a `try-except` block. This ensures that if the SQL query fails, the error is caught, and a message is displayed. An example of when a query would fail would be things like incorrect table names, network issues, or missing data. `st.stop()` is used to halt further execution of the app. Figure 8-5 shows how you can do this with the SQL query used in the first exercise in this chapter.

```
try:
    df = session.sql("SELECT * FROM SNOWFLAKE_SAMPLE_DATA.TPCH_SF1.NATIONS;").to_pandas()
    st.success("Data successfully loaded!")

except Exception as e:
    st.error(f"Query Execution Error: {str(e)}")
    st.stop()
```

Figure 8-5. *Wrapping a try-except block around our Snowflake query*

Streamlit Errors

After retrieving the data from Snowflake, `st.dataframe()` is used to display the dataframe in the Streamlit app. It is also wrapped in a `try-except` block to catch any potential rendering errors, such as issues with data formatting or visualization problems. In this case, if rendering fails (perhaps due to an invalid dataframe or an issue with Streamlit's internal handling), the error will be captured and displayed.

Chapter 8 Getting Started with Streamlit

```
try:
    # Render the dataframe again without the index column
    st.dataframe(df, hide_index=True)
except Exception as e:
    st.error(f"Streamlit Rendering Error: {str(e)}")
    st.stop()
```

Note There are other ways to handle errors in Streamlit besides using a `try-except` block. While `try-except` is the most common method, you can also use Streamlit's built-in functions and patterns to handle and display errors more effectively.

Summary

This chapter explained that Streamlit is a powerful Python library for creating interactive web applications with minimal coding expertise. You worked directly with Streamlit to build a basic app and then another app with dynamic filtering. The chapter also addressed best practices for error handling to ensure robust and reliable application performance. To dive deeper into the world of Streamlit, check out the tutorials that Snowflake has available at `https://docs.snowflake.com/en/tutorials`. You should now feel ready to develop and make some impactful data-driven web applications.

CHAPTER 9

Designing a Modern Analytics Solution with Snowflake

You are now familiar with the Snowflake data warehouse and its advantages over similar solutions. However, a typical organization won't be using Snowflake alone. Snowflake is part of an analytics solution that consists of multiple components, including business intelligence and data integration tools.

This chapter discusses a modern solution architecture and the role of Snowflake in it. It covers the following topics.

- Modern analytics solution architecture
- Snowflake partner ecosystem
- Integration with ETL/ELT and BI tools

The chapter explains how to build an end-to-end solution using leading cloud tools for business intelligence and data integration. There are lots of tools on the market. They can be divided into the following buckets.

- Low-code and no-code vs. code applications
- Open source software vs. commercial

CHAPTER 9 DESIGNING A MODERN ANALYTICS SOLUTION WITH SNOWFLAKE

Snowflake works equally well with low-code and open source applications.

You will launch Matillion ETL and load data into the Snowflake data warehouse, connect to Tableau Desktop, build dashboards, and learn about dbt and Airbyte.

Modern Analytics Solution Architecture

Nowadays, every organization wants to be data-driven to generate more value for customers and stakeholders. The organization's management understands the value of data and treats it as an asset. They are ready to invest in modern cloud solutions, such as Snowflake, that are scalable and secure. However, Snowflake is only one part of the analytical ecosystem. It is the core data storage for all organization data, and it provides robust access to the data.

You need more elements to build the right solution. These elements include data integration tools, business intelligence, and data modeling tools. Figure 9-1 highlights the key elements of a modern analytics solution.

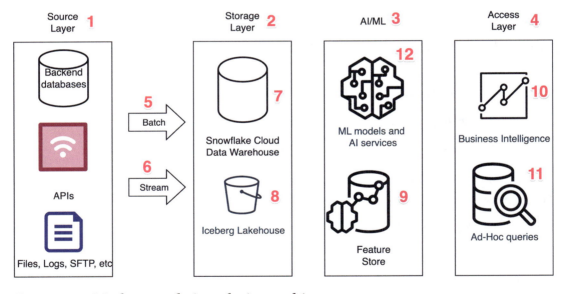

Figure 9-1. Modern analytics solution architecture

Figure 9-1 gives you an idea of how a typical analytics solution can look. I've already added Matillion ETL and Tableau to the diagram because we are going to use them in this chapter. However, you have a choice to use other products as welll.

Table 9-1 describes additional information for each element of the architecture.

Table 9-1. Key Elements of Architecture Diagram

Element	Description
Source layer	The source layer includes all the data sources available at your organization. This could include transactional databases, files, NoSQL databases, business applications, external APIs, sensors, and IoT.
Storage layer	The storage layer is the core of solution. You may hear about data platforms, data lakes, and data warehouses. This is the place for all of them. You are ingesting data into the storage layer from the source layers, and you store this data for further analysis, data discovery, or the decision-making process.
AI/ML layer	Dedicated layer for Machine Learning, Generative AI, and Data Science workloads and applications.
Access layer	The access layer is nontechnical. The main goal is to provide access for business users and allow them to interact with data through BI and SQL.
Stream	Streaming is a method of data ingesting using real-time data injection. For example, you can collect data from sensors, and you have a strict SLA to analyze the data and make decisions.
Batch	Batch Processing is a method of data ingesting. For example, for DWs, we load data once per day. Sometimes, we should load data more frequently.
Snowflake	Snowflake is cloud data warehouse that can serve as a data lake. It can collect data from both batching and streaming pipelines.
Iceberg Lakehouse	Data platform with raw data in Iceberg format
Feature Store	Dedicated data marts for Machine learning models.
Business Intelligence	Visual analytics tools that connects to Snowflake and provides access for the business users and helps them slice/dice data and deliver insights. In other words, it is business intelligence tool.
Ad-hoc queries	Custom SQL and Python scripts to query Snowflake data platform.
Data science tools	Data science tools provide advanced analytics capabilities. It could be an open source product, programming language (R/Python), or enterprise solution like Spark Databricks.

CHAPTER 9   DESIGNING A MODERN ANALYTICS SOLUTION WITH SNOWFLAKE

In this chapter, we will show how to build simple solutions using Matillion ETL, Snowflake, and Tableau. We won't spend much time on setting up a real source system and will use sample data sets that we will load into Snowflake with Matillion and then visualize with Tableau. Moreover, we won't build a streaming solution or talk about lambda architecture. Based on our experience in 80 percent of use cases, using a data warehouse, business intelligence, and ELT is sufficient for a typical organization.

Snowflake Partner Ecosystem

Snowflake has many technology partners, and it provides good integration with them. In addition, it has a convenient feature called Partner Connect that allows you to launch a solution via the Snowflake web interface, as shown in Figure 9-2.

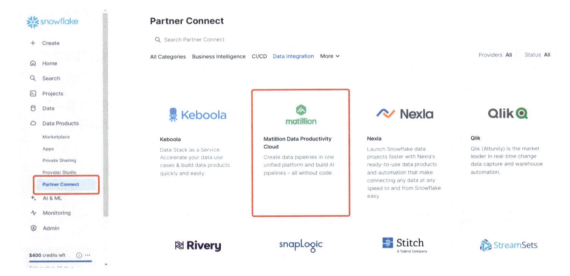

Figure 9-2. *Snowflake Partner Connect page*

Moreover, Snowflake provides native drivers like JDBC, ODBC, and others for connecting to third-party tools such as Tableau, SqlDBM, Spark, and others. Figure 9-3 shows the list of available drivers. Go to `www.snowflake.com/en/`, and select Developers ➤ Downloads to get to this menu.

CHAPTER 9 DESIGNING A MODERN ANALYTICS SOLUTION WITH SNOWFLAKE

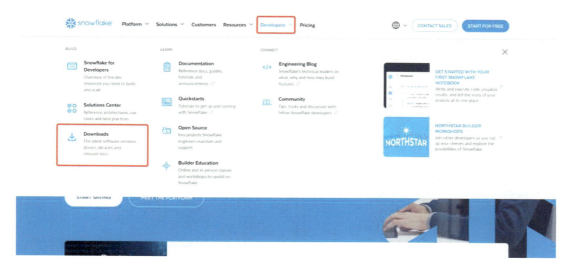

Figure 9-3. *Snowflake drivers*

Our solution needs a data integration tool and a business intelligence (BI) tool. Based on our rich experience with data warehouses, BI, and data integration, our favorite tools for working with Snowflake are Matillion ETL and Tableau. They are leaders in their area and allow building a modern analytics solution and meet business requirements and SLAs.

Building Analytics Solutions with Matillion ETL and Tableau

This solution demonstrates the use of commercial tools integrated with Snowflake, such as Tableau and Matillion. For the purposes of this book, we will leverage their free trial versions to walk through practical examples.

Getting Started with Matillion ETL

Matillion ETL is cloud data integration tool. It is available for Snowflake, Redshift, and BigQuery. It increases development speed, secures data, provides rich data transformation functionality, and offers many prebuilt data connectors for Salesforce, Mailchimp, Facebook, and others. One of the biggest advantages of the tool is that it looks and feels like a traditional ETL tool with a friendly user interface where developers can drag and drop components to build their data pipeline.

149

CHAPTER 9   DESIGNING A MODERN ANALYTICS SOLUTION WITH SNOWFLAKE

To start with Matillion ETL, click the Matillion box shown in Figure 9-2. This will open a new window and ask permission to create objects within a Snowflake account. You can see the list of objects in Table 9-2.

Table 9-2. List of Matillion Objects

Object	Object
Database	PC_MATILLION_DB
Warehouse	PC_MATILLION_WH (X-Small)
Role	PC_MATILLION_ROLE
Username	Snowflake-snowflake

After activation, the tool will immediately transfer you to the Matillion ETL web interface. This is connected to your Snowflake cluster, and you may start to work immediately. This decrease your time to market.

Let's load some initial data into Snowflake using Matillion.

Note Our Snowflake cluster is hosted on AWS. When we launched a Matillion ETL instance from the Partner Connect page, we created the EC2 instance with Matillion ETL. It was created in a different AWS account. We can launch Matillion ETL in our AWS account by finding it in the AWS Marketplace.

RUNNING OUR FIRST JOB WITH MATILLION ETL

We will use a demo Matillion ETL job and sample airport data in order to create our first ELT job and then load and transform data for our Snowflake DW. Let's get started.

1. Log into Matillion ETL. You can use the URL, password, and username that you've received in the Matillion activation e-mail.

2. Navigate to Designer ➤ Snowflake Project. You will a demo job called GreenWave Pipelines.

CHAPTER 9   DESIGNING A MODERN ANALYTICS SOLUTION WITH SNOWFLAKE

3. Open the GreenWave Technologies Demo job by clicking it twice. In Figure 9-4, we are showing key elements of the Matillion web interface.

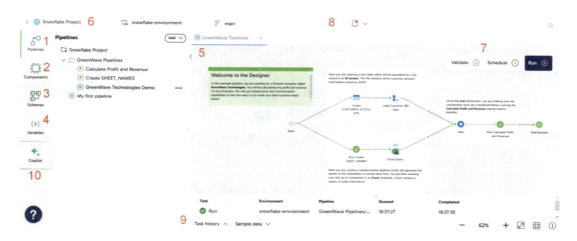

Figure 9-4. Matillion Pipeline example

When you are working with Matillion, you are working mostly from a browser. The same is true for Snowflake. Table 9-3 describes the key elements of the Matillion ETL web interface shown in Figure 9-4.

Table 9-3. Key Elements of Matillion ETL Web Interface

Element in Figure 9-4	Description
1	Pipelines panel (Files panel) — shows all orchestration/transformation pipelines and folders in your project.
2	Components panel — lists available components (connectors, flow logic, iterators) specific to the pipeline type.
3	Schemas panel — lets you browse database schemas, including tables, views, and other metadata.
4	Variables panel — displays pipeline and project variables (text, number, grid) for parameterizing jobs.

(continued)

CHAPTER 9   DESIGNING A MODERN ANALYTICS SOLUTION WITH SNOWFLAKE

Table 9-3. (*continued*)

Element in Figure 9-4	Description
5	Designer canvas — the central workspace where components are dragged, arranged, and connected.
6	Project / environment / branch info — shows project name (e.g. "Snowflake Project"), selected environment, and current Git branch.
7	Pipeline controls ("Validate", "Schedule", "Run") — buttons to validate the pipeline, set schedules, and execute runs.
8	From the pane you can work with version control by commiting changes, pull or push changes ect.
9	Task history and Sample data panes are for monitoring and managing the execution of your ETL jobs.
10	With Copilot, you can create data pipelines simply using plain language instructions.

You have learned about the key elements of the Matillion web interface, so you can now run a job. Click the **Run** button on the canvas. Matillion runs the current job using the environment named *Snowflake*. This job consists of multiple steps.

  a. Create tables using the Create Table component.
  b. Load data from S3 into the staging tables using the S3 Load component.
  c. Execute the GreenWave Technologies Demo transformation job that transforms raw semi-structured data into a tabular format and loads it into a dimension table.

Note   This exercise loads the Matillion sample dataset that is stored in an Amazon S3 bucket. This bucket is public and is available to everyone. If you have Snowflake on Azure, then you load data from Blob Storage.

CHAPTER 9   DESIGNING A MODERN ANALYTICS SOLUTION WITH SNOWFLAKE

4. After the job is finished, go back to the Snowflake web UI and check the new objects that were created by Matillion. Figure 9-5 shows the list of Snowflake tables that were created by the Matillion orchestration job.

Figure 9-5. Snowflake tables created by Matillion ETL

We launched Matillion ETL and loaded sample data into the Snowflake data warehouse. In a real-world scenario, you would create many more jobs and collect data from external sources. For example, for marketing analytics use cases, you need to load data from social media platforms such as Facebook, Twitter, YouTube, and so on. Matillion ETL provides prebuilt connectors that save time for data engineers or ETL developers.

Moreover, for a quality solution, you should design a data model for querying our data. You might choose a technique like using Data Vault, dimensional modeling, and so on. The best choice for the Snowflake data model is SqlDBM.

The final step is to connect to a BI tool for simplifying access for nontechnical users. With Tableau, business users can do data discovery using drag-and-drop methods and powerful analytics and visualization capabilities. For our sample solution, we installed Tableau Desktop and connected it to the CUSTOMER_ACCOUNT table to visualize data.

153

CHAPTER 9 DESIGNING A MODERN ANALYTICS SOLUTION WITH SNOWFLAKE

Getting Started with Tableau

Tableau is a leading visual analytics platform. There are many tools available on the market, but Tableau stands out among them. We have worked with many different tools from leading vendors and found that Tableau is the most powerful tool for business intelligence and self-service. Moreover, it has a large and friendly community. If you have never worked with Tableau, now is a good time to try it. Connecting Tableau to Snowflake allows you to use best-of-breed technologies working together. Tableau is available in server and desktop versions. Moreover, it has a mobile application. Let's get Tableau and connect to the Snowflake cluster.

> **BUILDING OUR FIRST VISUALIZATION WITH TABLEAU AND SNOWFLAKE**
>
> This exercise installs Tableau Desktop and connects it to the Snowflake data warehouse. Then, you can visualize the CUSTOMER_ACCOUNT data.
>
> 1. Let's download and install Tableau Desktop. Go to www.tableau.com/products/desktop/download and download a recent version of Tableau Desktop. It is available for macOS and Windows. Then install it.
>
> 2. Open Tableau Desktop and connect to Snowflake, as shown in Figure 9-6.
>
>

Figure 9-6. Tableau Desktop connection to Snowflake

CHAPTER 9 DESIGNING A MODERN ANALYTICS SOLUTION WITH SNOWFLAKE

Note To connect to the Snowflake data warehouse, you need to download the ODBC driver from www.snowflake.com/en/developers/downloads/odbc/. Download it and install it.

3. Then, you should enter your credentials to connect to Snowflake from Tableau. You can use the Matillion credentials that were created during the Matillion ETL initializing, including the user role, or you can use your master credentials. You should use your admin Snowflake credentials. Figure 9-7 shows an example of the connection options.

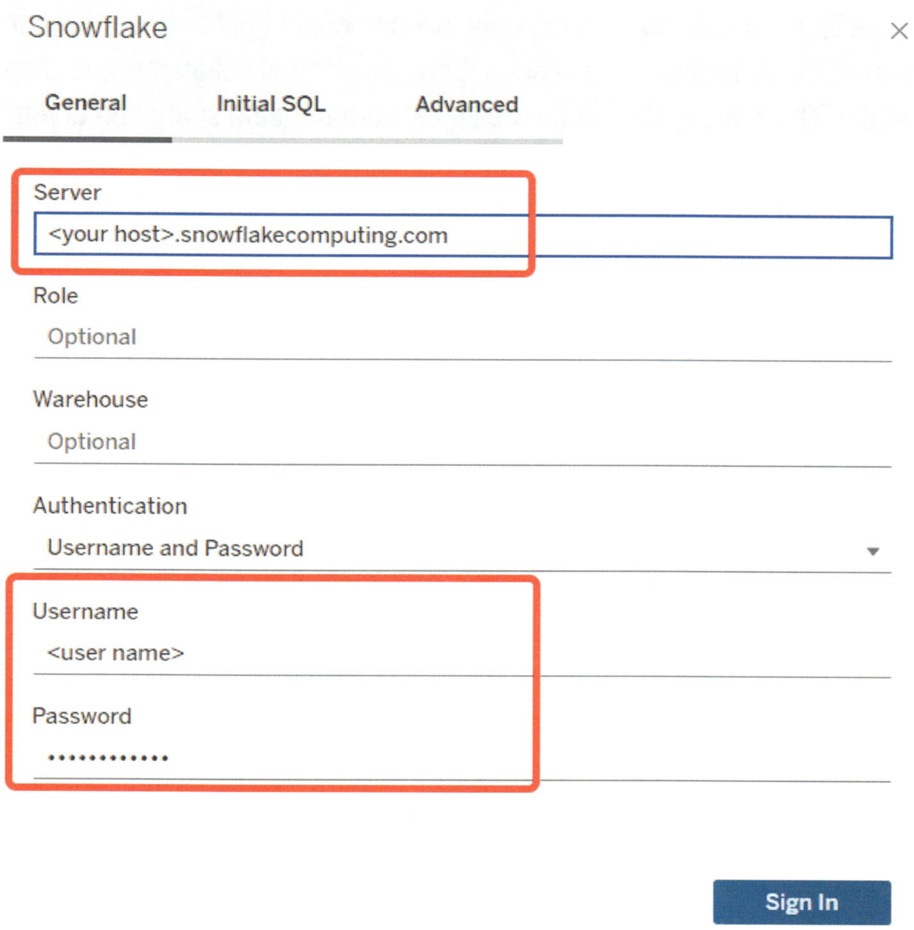

Figure 9-7. Snowflake connection window

CHAPTER 9   DESIGNING A MODERN ANALYTICS SOLUTION WITH SNOWFLAKE

4. Click **Sign In** and then enter the following.

    a. Warehouse: PC_MATILLIONLOADER_WH

    b. Database: PC_MATILLIONLOADER_DB

    c. Schema: Public

    Then, drag and drop the CUSTOMER_ACCOUNT table to the connection canvas.

5. Click **Sheet 1** to jump into the development area. You just created your first Tableau live data source.

Note   The Tableau data source supports live and extract options. Extract queries all data from the data source and cache it into an internal columnar data store called Hyper. The live connection queries data from the data source on demand. This is the right strategy for a big volume of data. With a live connection, Snowflake does the heavy lifting, and Tableau renders the result. This is the secret to doing big data analytics.

---

6. Let's create a quick visualization using the available data. Suppose you want to know how many clients were born in the US. Figure 9-8 shows the Tableau Desktop interface and a simple report.

CHAPTER 9   DESIGNING A MODERN ANALYTICS SOLUTION WITH SNOWFLAKE

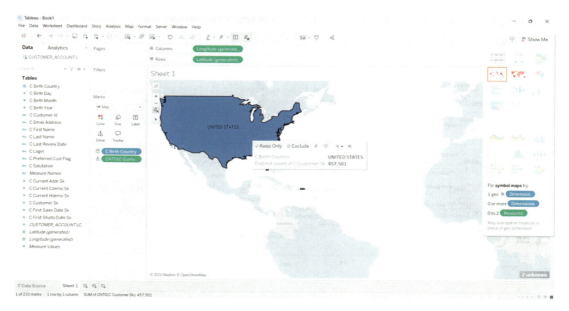

Figure 9-8. Tableau sheet

We built this report by dragging and dropping the (blue) Birth Country dimension into the Rows pane and Calculated Field #Customer Sk into the Columns pane. To create a calculated field, click the right button in the Measures pane and choose **Create Calculated Field**.

This counts the distinct (unique) number of customers.

7. It is interesting to look at Snowflake to see what was happening when we built our report. From the Snowflake web UI on the History tab, you can see the SQL query that was generated by Tableau.

```
SELECT "CUSTOMER_ACCOUNT"."C_BIRTH_COUNTRY" AS "C_BIRTH_
COUNTRY",
  COUNT(DISTINCT "CUSTOMER_ACCOUNT"."C_CUSTOMER_SK") AS "ctd:C_
  CUSTOMER_SK:ok"
FROM "PC_MATILLIONLOADER_DB"."PUBLIC"."CUSTOMER_ACCOUNT"
"CUSTOMER_ACCOUNT"
GROUP BY 1
```

157

Moreover, you can look at the execution plan. This is helpful when working with large datasets and multiple tables.

We connected the Snowflake data warehouse with Tableau Desktop. The next logical step is to publish the report to the Tableau server and share it with stakeholders.

Note With Tableau, you can leverage the unique features of Snowflake such as querying and visualizing semi-structured data, working with the Time Travel feature, sharing data, implementing role-based security, and using custom aggregation.

Building Analytics Solution with Open Source Software

You learned about the option of building a low-code data analytics solution using Matillion ETL and Tableau. This might be an excellent choice for a company with an established data team and a budget to cover licensing costs. However, for small companies or startups, this isn't a feasible option. They are often restricted by budget constraints and are looking for open source alternatives. Snowflake remains a great choice, as it has already proven itself to be effective for many small companies and startups.

This section of the chapter discusses open source alternatives for BI and data integration/transformation. In the previous example, Matillion ETL handled both data ingestion and transformations. Now, let's split these use cases and identify the right tools for each task. Table 9-4 lists tasks and potential open source tools.

Table 9-4. *Available Tools for Tasks*

Task	Available Tools
Data ingestion	Airbyte, Meltano, Python Code
Data transformation	dbt Core, Python libraries, Apache Spark
Data orchestration	Apache Airflow, Prefect, Dagster, Luigi, cron
Business intelligence	Metabase, Redash, Apache Superset

There are many open source tools available in the market. Python can also be used. Alternatively, you can choose any other programming language to create custom tools. However, this approach is not scalable, is difficult to maintain, and often serves as an anti-pattern.

Each tool and approach has its own pros and cons. Before selecting any particular technology, you should typically run a proof of concept (PoC) and compile a list of use cases and scenarios to evaluate potential candidates. The outcome of the PoC should be a document highlighting the winner of the selection process, as well as details on costs, effort, and other relevant factors. This document helps with making an informed decision and securing approval from the executive team.

This exercise attempts to create a simple solution using dbt Core and Snowflake. We discuss end-to-end solution options but not in detail.

There are many options for hosting open source solutions in a production environment, which are often tied to managed Kubernetes clusters or container services provided by public cloud vendors such as AWS, Azure, or GCP.

Figure 9-9 outlines the high-level architecture of the solution.

CHAPTER 9   DESIGNING A MODERN ANALYTICS SOLUTION WITH SNOWFLAKE

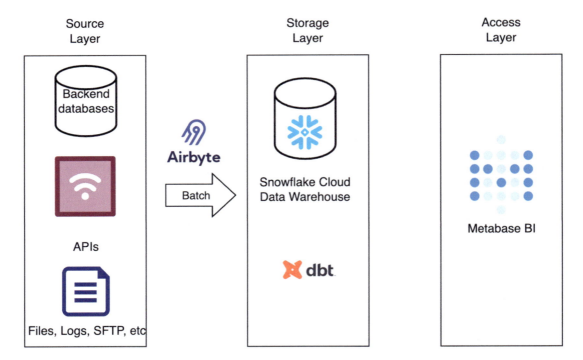

Figure 9-9. Architecture

First, make sure you have a trial or real account of Snowflake. If you still don't have it, feel free to create it at https://signup.snowflake.com/.

Figure 9-9 shows an open source version of Airbyte for data ingestion. The primary goal of Airbyte is data ingestion. It has a nice UI and lots of connectors to different applications such as Salesforce, Google Analytics, and Amplitude, with the ability to write data into Snowflake, BigQuery, Redshift, and so on.

If you want to add Airbyte, you can install it locally using the Airbyte command-line tool (https://docs.airbyte.com/using-airbyte/getting-started/oss-quickstart) or using minikube and Helm charts (https://artifacthub.io/packages/helm/airbyte/airbyte). You can find more details in this chapter's repository.

Apache Airflow is the most popular Python-based orchestration tool that can execute our pipelines and jobs with Direct Acyclic Graphs. You can install Airflow locally using multiple options, including Helm values (https://airflow.apache.org/docs/apache-airflow/stable/installation/index.html).

Metabase is a popular SQL-based BI tool. This chapter runs Metabase in a Docker container to connect Snowflake.

CHAPTER 9   DESIGNING A MODERN ANALYTICS SOLUTION WITH SNOWFLAKE

dbt Core is the most powerful and popular framework for data transformation inside your data warehouse. Usually, it works together with data ingestion software like Airbyte and Fivetran. As soon as data is ingested into a data warehouse, you can model it. DBT has lots of advantages.

- Creates a unified SQL framework
- Transforms business login into SQL
- Allows application software engineering principles such as continuous integration/continuous deployment, unit testing, pre-commit, version control, blue-green deployment
- Easy to learn and maintain
- Allows to create reusable code snipes with Jinja macros
- Out-of-the-box development/production environment split
- Gives the option to write vendor-agnostic SQL queries that allow migration from one vendor to another

Although we covered key tools for open source alternatives, Airbyte or Airflow aren't used in our example because it could be tricky to reproduce. The GitHub repo highlights the steps to deploy it locally.

Let's review the typical deployment process for a prototype. There are a couple options for local deployment.

- Using Docker Compose
- Using minikube

The choice depends on your preference and production deployment plans. For example, with Docker containers, you can deploy everything on AWS Elastic Container Services or similar alternatives in Azure and Google Cloud. When using Helm values, you can deploy everything to the minikube or Kubernetes cluster in the cloud.

Running a dbt Project

As a starting point, you can clone the repo with materials. Examples are shared on macOS. If you are using Windows OS, the command would be different. The workaround could be using the free GitHub Codespaces (https://github.com/features/codespaces) as a cloud IDE.

Clone the repo into a local machine using this command in your IDE of choice.

```
git clone <Book Repo>
cd <Book Repo Folder>/chapter_9/
# if you don't have virtual env, we need to create one
# ucomment following command
# python3 -m venv venv
source venv/bin/activate
pip install -r requirements.txt
```

This installs dbt Core for Snowflake. In `requirements.txt`, there are two key packages related to this.

- dbt-core==1.8.7
- dbt-snowflake==1.8.3

Let's test that the dbt is installed.

```
dbt --version
Core:
  - installed: 1.8.7
Plugins:
  - snowflake: 1.8.3
```

This repository already has a dbt project. First, open the /chapter_9/01_setup.sql file. This query does the following.

- Creates a new user `dbt_user`
- Creates a new role `jumpstart_admin`
- Creates a new warehouse `xscompute`
- Creates a new database `jumpstart`

- Creates new schemas `business` and `stg`
- Grants permissions for accessing Snowflake Sample data

You can find the dbt profile in the `chapter_9/snowflakebook/` folder. Place it in the default location: the `~/.dbt` folder.

`cp profiles.yml ~/.dbt/profiles.yml`

The dbt project is in the `snowflakebook` folder, which was created using the `dbt init` command. You can create your own project in another folder if you want to start from scratch.

You need to connect to Snowflake to build dbt models. Dbt model contains SQL logic for data transformations. During the model run, dbt compiles SQL and sends it to Snowflake for execution.

Let's review the components of the dbt project.

- `dbt_project.yml` is the main configuration file.
- The `models` folder contains dbt models. Each dbt model is a SQL file (i.e., transformation).
- `profiles.yml` defines the connection to Snowflake or any other data warehouse platform. This file was used to copy into `~/.dbt/profiles.yml`.

Before you can run our models, you need to make sure dbt is connected to the Snowflake. For this purpose, you should make sure you have a proper dbt profile. It requires the `SNOWFLAKE_ACCOUNT` variable. You have to export it.

`export SNOWFLAKE_ACCOUNT=<YOUR_ACCOUNT>`

Our example used ah459331.east-us-2.azure.

Test your connection to Snowflake by running the `dbt debug` command; it should return "All checks passed!" This means you are good to go with dbt model development.

Note One of the advantages of dbt is a local development environment. It allows you to easily split the production and development environment to test and build models in the development schema without any risk of breaking the production environment. Environments are configured in `profiles.yml`.

After testing the connection, you should run `dbt deps` to install all dbt packages from `packages.yml`. There are lots of useful packages available in the dbt hub (https://hub.getdbt.com).

Typical dbt projects consist of layers. You can leverage the approach of Medallion architecture with `bronze`, `silver`, and `gold` subfolders, or you can use anything you like. In our case, we defined two layers in the Snowflake warehouse: `stg` as the staging layer and `business` as a layer for fact tables. The folder structure is for our convenience. You should match the folders in models with the `dbt_project.yml` file.

You can check the staging models in `/chapter_9/snowflakebook/models/staging`. Based on the `dbt_project.yml` config, we chose `+materialized: view` (i.e., Snowflake creates views). But there is an option to create a table. Moreover, in production, we usually use different incremental models to avoid expensive reloads of data.

To run all our models and corresponding data tests, you can use the `dbt build` command. Alternatively, you can run only the models with `dbt run` or only the tests with `dbt test`. Moreover, you can run a given model with the `dbt run --select <MODEL>` command. In other words, Snowflake is creating a SQL query based on dbt models and executing it on the Snowflake side.

Briefly speaking, a dbt is a SQL framework that allows you to convert business logic into SQL dbt models with dependencies, data tests, and documentation; it is easy to use and onboard. A dbt doesn't do any heavy lifting. You can review the SQL commands it generates in `/chapter_9/snowflakebook/target` or review logs in `/chapter_9/snowflakebook/logs/dbt.log`.

The dbt run should create views in the jumpstart database. Figure 9-10 shows an example.

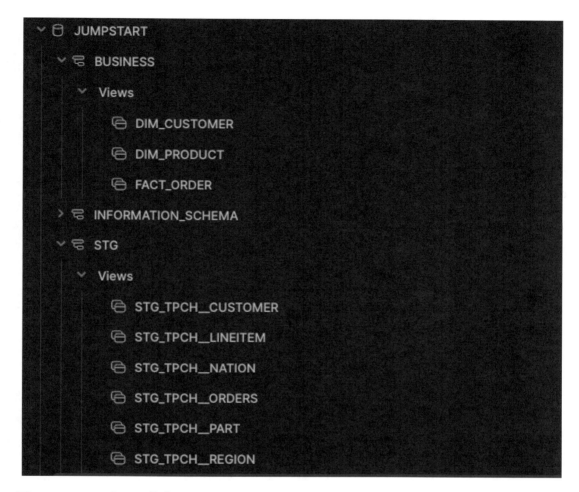

Figure 9-10. Snowflake views

Next, you can deploy Metabase BI and connect to Snowflake using the same `dbt_user`.

Metabase is a popular BI tool. It allows you to connect data warehouse and write SQL queries using browser. It is different from Tableau, where you can drag-and-drop dimensions and measure to build a dashboard. In Metabase, you should write a SQL for each table of visual element and then combine elements together in a dashboard.

It is available as managed version that isn't free or community edition that is free. Usually, Metabase is deployed in the container and might be hosted in container services like AWS Elastic Container Service and Azure Kubernetes Service.

Metabase is a great choice for a small company or as a complimentary BI tool for tools like Tableau and Looker.

CHAPTER 9   DESIGNING A MODERN ANALYTICS SOLUTION WITH SNOWFLAKE

In the book repository, you can see the command to pull the last Metabase image and start the container /chapter_9/readme.md

Let's run several commands in our terminal. It requires to run Docker Desktop application.

```
# pull last official image with metabase
docker pull metabase/metabase:latest
```

```
# start metabase container on port 3000
docker run -d -p 3000:3000 --name metabase metabase/metabase
```

Go to http://localhost:3000 in a browser to open Metabase. You can register with your email address, and you are ready to connect to the Snowflake data warehouse.

In Metabase, you can review sample dashboards in the Example collection at http://localhost:3000/collection/2-examples.

Go to the Admin console at http://localhost:3000/admin/databases, and click **Add Database**. Choose **Snowflake** and enter the credentials for your Snowflake instance. You can use the same user and password that we used for dbt.

Ideally, in a production environment, every service should have its own user, role, and compute warehouse.

After establishing a connection with Snowflake, you are ready to write SQL queries and turn them into visuals.

Go back to the home page (http://localhost:3000/), and in the top-right corner, click **New**. It opens a window where you can insert a SQL query. You can get the SQL query from the GitHub repo at /chapter_9/readme.md. Figure 9-11 is a screenshot from Metabase.

CHAPTER 9 DESIGNING A MODERN ANALYTICS SOLUTION WITH SNOWFLAKE

Figure 9-11. Metabase example

Metabase allows you to explore data, build visuals, and combine them into dashboards with filters and parameters for self-service BI. Another advantage of Metabase is API that allows you to programmatically execute reports from ETL tools, getting data or visuals and sending them over email or messengers, with a community edition, everything for free except engineering labor.

Engineering Excellence with dbt Development

Before wrapping the chapter, we want to give you some guidance on best practices for working with dbt. Since dbt allows you to work with code, you can leverage best practices of software engineering such as pre-commit, CI/CD, containerization, unit tests, and so on.

Typically, dbt code and modules are stored in the git version system. Before starting work on development, you should create a development branch. For example, `git checkout feature/new-dbt-model`. This command creates a development branch for us.

You can modify our existing code or add a new code. When done, we usually commit and push the code for code review. It is good practice to use pre-commit to automatically check with code before sharing it with the team. You can learn more about pre-commit at https://pre-commit.com.

CHAPTER 9   DESIGNING A MODERN ANALYTICS SOLUTION WITH SNOWFLAKE

Let's first review the pre-commit specifically for dbt and Snowflake. The repo provides an example of a pre-commit config for dbt and Snowflake. You can find this in the root directory as well as the dbt project /chapter_9/.pre-commit-config.yaml. Table 9-5 describes each hook.

Table 9-5. *Pre-Commit Hooks*

Hook	Description
trailing-whitespace	Removes unnecessary whitespace at the end of lines to maintain clean and consistent code formatting
check-yaml	Validates YAML files to ensure they are syntactically correct and well-formed
prettier	Automatically formats code to enforce a consistent style across various programming languages and file types
black	Provides an opinionated Python code formatter that automatically resolves code style and formatting issues
flake8	Checks Python code for style guide enforcement (PEP 8) and identifies potential errors or code quality issues
dbt-checkpoint	Runs additional checks and validations specific to dbt (data build tool) projects to maintain code quality and best practices
sqlfluff	Automatically fixes SQL code to ensure consistent formatting and detect potential SQL syntax problems

Pre-commit is already installed with requirements.txt, and you can activate it by running the following.

```
pre-commit install
```

You also need to make sure to provide the SQLFluff config file. We provided .sqlfluff in the repo.

You can run pre-commit with git commands.

```
git add .
git commit -m "Update dbt model"
```

Alternatively, you can run the following.

```
pre-commit run --all-files
```

CHAPTER 9 DESIGNING A MODERN ANALYTICS SOLUTION WITH SNOWFLAKE

This runs our pre-commit hooks for the changed file. dbt models already linted with SQLFluff.

This is a great example of how to enforce the quality of dbt and data engineering quality.

Data Ingestion and Orchestration

Our example used dbt on top of available data in Snowflake data share sample data. In a real-world scenario, you would need to ingest data into Snowflake.

For ingestion data, you may consider Airbyte or Meltano to deploy. Our example uses Airbyte.

Airbyte offers hundreds of connectors to source applications, databases, and APIs such as Postgres, Salesforce, Amplitude, and so on. Airbyte gives provides a user interface. It looks and feels similar to Fivetran.

There are two options available for deploying Airbyte.

- The Airbyte command-line tool (`aclt`)
- A Helm chart to deploy on minikube or Kubernetes cluster

You can check the examples for deploying Airbyte with `aclt` and a Helm chart at `chapter_9/readme.md`.

Let's review an example of installing the Airbyte on a local minikube.

> **Note** minikube is a lightweight Kubernetes implementation that lets you run a single-node Kubernetes cluster locally for development and testing purposes. You can learn how to install it locally using the guide at `https://minikube.sigs.k8s.io/docs/start/`.

Once minikube is installed, the next step is to start it.

`minikube start`

Helm and kubectl are also needed.

Helm is a package manager for Kubernetes that simplifies the deployment and management of applications by using *charts*, which are pre-configured Kubernetes resources. You can learn how to install it locally at `https://github.com/helm/helm`

kubectl is the command-line tool used to interact with a Kubernetes cluster, allowing you to deploy, inspect, manage, and troubleshoot resources and applications within the cluster. minikube is a lightweight Kubernetes implementation that lets you run a single-node Kubernetes cluster locally for development and testing purposes. You can learn how to install it locally using the guide at https://kubernetes.io/docs/tasks/tools/.

```
helm repo add airbyte https://airbytehq.github.io/helm-charts

helm install airbyte airbyte/airbyte --version 1.2.0
```

The output should be similar to the following.

```
NAMESPACE: default
STATUS: deployed
REVISION: 1
NOTES:
1. Get the application URL by running these commands:
  export POD_NAME=$(kubectl get pods --namespace default -l "app.kubernetes.io/name=webapp" -o jsonpath="{.items[0].metadata.name}")
  export CONTAINER_PORT=$(kubectl get pod --namespace default $POD_NAME -o jsonpath="{.spec.containers[0].ports[0].containerPort}")
  echo "Visit http://127.0.0.1:8080 to use your application"
  kubectl --namespace default port-forward $POD_NAME 8080:$CONTAINER_PORT
```

Open Airbyte at http://localhost:8080.

Using the same minikube cluster, add the Airflow Helm chart.

```
helm repo add apache-airflow https://airflow.apache.org
helm upgrade --install airflow apache-airflow/airflow --namespace airflow --create-namespace
```

You can learn more about this in Airflow documentation at https://airflow.apache.org/docs/helm-chart/stable/index.html. If you are using Airflow hosted on Kubernetes, you should run dbt in KubernetesPodOperator. Every Airflow dbt DAG starts a new pod with a dbt image and runs dbt models in it. You can learn about dbt and Airflow in the article at www.astronomer.io/blog/airflow-and-dbt/.

To summarize, you can build a data stack for the Snowflake data warehouse using open source tools for data ingestion, transformation, and orchestration. One of the best options to deploy your open source stack is to run it on a Kubernetes cluster.

In addition, you can add tools for data observability, monitoring, and data governance using Helm charts and deploy them on Kubernetes.

Summary

This chapter covered the Snowflake partner ecosystem. You learned about modern analytics architecture and its key elements. You connected to the best cloud ELT tool for Snowflake, Matillion ETL, and ran our first job. Then, you built a report with the Tableau visual analytics tool and discovered the open source data stack. You also learned about dbt Core, Metabase, Airbyte, and Airflow.

The next chapter discusses performance optimization and cost monitoring in Snowflake.

CHAPTER 10

Performance Optimization and Cost Monitoring

Snowflake is a powerful, cloud-native data platform designed to support a wide variety of data workloads, from interactive analytics to batch processing and everything in between. But getting the best performance and value from Snowflake isn't automatic—it requires a clear understanding of how Snowflake works under the hood and how to make the most of its optimization features.

This chapter walks through practical strategies for improving the efficiency, speed, and cost-effectiveness of your Snowflake environment. Whether you're working with large datasets, designing data pipelines, or managing compute resources, these recipes help you fine-tune your setup for real-world demands.

You'll learn how to do the following.

- Understand and optimize data reads using clustering, partition pruning, and pruning-aware data loading
- Improve data processing performance through query design and task tuning
- Configure and scale virtual warehouses effectively to balance performance and cost
- Monitor and control resource consumption to avoid unexpected costs and inefficiencies

By the end of this chapter, you'll be equipped with actionable techniques to get the most out of Snowflake's performance capabilities—whether you're a data engineer, architect, or platform owner.

Understanding Snowflake Architecture for Optimization

Snowflake's architecture is built on a separation of compute and storage, offering distinct advantages for performance and cost control. To optimize effectively, you must understand its key architectural features.

- **Virtual warehouses**: Compute resources used for query execution. Warehouses can be scaled up (more power) or out (more parallelism) as needed. In Snowflake, this can be managed through the web interface, SQL commands, or the Snowflake REST API. To scale up, you can choose a larger warehouse size (e.g., XS to M) for increased compute power. To scale out, you can enable multi-cluster warehouses, allowing Snowflake to add additional clusters automatically based on query concurrency. For example, for a small analytics task, an XS warehouse might suffice, but a L or XL warehouse is more suitable for processing terabytes of data in parallel.

- **Centralized storage**: Shared, cloud-based storage layer accessible by all virtual warehouses. Data in Snowflake is stored in a centralized repository using cloud-based object storage (e.g., AWS S3, Azure Blob Storage, or Google Cloud Storage). Multiple teams can work on different virtual warehouses accessing the same dataset stored centrally without duplication.

- **Cloud services layer**: This layer manages metadata, query parsing, optimization, authentication, and security. It acts as the "brain" of Snowflake's architecture, coordinating operations across the storage and compute layers. Features like automatic query optimization and metadata-driven partition pruning are managed here. Snowflake automates tasks like clustering and indexing, reducing administrative overhead.

The Snowflake performance optimization techniques broadly fall into three separate categories.

- Data read optimization
- Data processing optimization
- Warehouse configuration optimization

Data Read Optimization

Data Clustering and Partitioning

Efficient data reading in Snowflake is largely driven by its automatic micro-partitioning system and optional clustering. These features work together to reduce the amount of data scanned during queries, improving performance and minimizing compute cost.

- **Micro-partitioning overview**

    When data is loaded into a Snowflake table, it is automatically divided into micro-partitions—contiguous units of storage typically containing 50 MB to 500 MB of compressed data. Each partition stores rich column-level metadata, including min/max values, null counts, and more.

    Snowflake uses this metadata to skip scanning irrelevant partitions during query execution—a technique known as *partition pruning*. This behavior is automatic and requires no manual configuration.

- **Clustering keys**

    - For large tables where query performance is critical, you can define clustering keys to influence how data is physically organized across micro-partitions.

    - Choose columns frequently used in filters, JOINs, or GROUP BY clauses (e.g., transaction_date, region_id).

    - Avoid using high-cardinality columns (e.g., UUIDs, unique IDs) as clustering keys, as they may lead to inefficient or ineffective clustering.

- Clustering is especially beneficial for time-series, event, and large fact tables where filtering on a specific range or subset is common.

- **Monitoring clustering effectiveness**

    You can assess how well a table is clustered using the function.

    ```
    SELECT SYSTEM$CLUSTERING_INFORMATION('your_table_name');
    ```

    This returns metrics such as clustering depth, which indicates how well data aligns with the clustering keys. A higher depth may signal that the clustering has degraded over time due to new data inserts or updates.

    For tables with manual clustering (clustering defined but automatic clustering not enabled), you can use ALTER TABLE RECLUSTER to reorganize the data.

- **Sorting data during loading**

    Sorting data on clustering key columns before loading into Snowflake can improve query performance by ensuring that related records are stored together in the same micro-partitions. This approach is often referred to as natural clustering.

    You can apply this technique by using the SORT BY clause in the COPY INTO command or by pre-sorting the data in your ETL/ELT process. For example, sorting sales data by region and order_date ensures that queries filtering by these columns scan fewer micro-partitions and return results faster.

    While this method doesn't replace defined clustering keys, it complements them by improving the initial physical layout of the data.

- **Automatic clustering**

    Snowflake offers an automatic clustering feature that continuously manages partition organization as new data is added.

- Once enabled, Snowflake automatically reclusters the table based on the defined clustering keys; no manual action is required.

- This feature incurs additional cost, so it should be evaluated based on workload needs and query patterns.

- **Best practices for partitioning large datasets**

  - For time-series data, use date, datetime, or timestamp columns as clustering keys to optimizing range queries (e.g., by month or year).

  - For multi-dimensional filters, combine multiple columns in the clustering key, such as region, product_id, and transaction_date.

  - Monitor performance and clustering depth regularly, especially on large or fast-changing tables.

Data Storage Best Practices

Store only the data you need and use Snowflake's compression to minimize storage costs.

- **TIME TRAVEL**: This feature allows you to access historical data for a defined period (up to 90 days, depending on your Snowflake edition). You can query, restore, or clone data from a specific point in the past. It is useful for correcting accidental deletions or updates. The following is an example of recovering a deleted table. Useful for correcting accidental deletions or updates.

  ```
  SELECT * FROM sales AT (TIMESTAMP => '2025-01-01 10:00:00');
  ```

- **FAIL-SAFE**: This is the seven-day recovery period after TIME TRAVEL expires, designed for disaster recovery. Data in fail-safe is only accessible by Snowflake support and incurs additional costs. It acts as a safety net for critical data recovery.

CHAPTER 10 PERFORMANCE OPTIMIZATION AND COST MONITORING

Data Processing Optimization

Optimizing query performance is critical for reducing execution times and ensuring efficient resource utilization. Snowflake provides several tools and techniques to streamline queries.

Analyze Query Execution

Snowflake provides tools like Query Profile to analyze execution plans.

- Identify bottlenecks such as large table scans or inefficient joins.
- Optimize join order by ensuring smaller datasets are processed first.
- Avoid repeated computation by materializing intermediate results using temporary tables.

The following are some key metrics to examine.

- **Elapsed time**: Total time taken for query execution.
- **Partition scanning**: Number of partitions scanned during execution.
- **Processing steps**: Identify stages with high execution times.

One example would be a query scanning millions of partitions without proper filtering, which might indicate missing WHERE clauses or improperly clustered data.

Optimization Techniques

– **Prune unnecessary data**. Use filters and WHERE clauses to reduce scanned data. For example, querying specific date ranges reduces unnecessary data reads.

```
SELECT *
FROM sales
WHERE region = 'EMEA' AND sales_date >= '2024-01-01';
```

- **Avoid SELECT * statements.** Instead, specify required columns explicitly to reduce data transfer and processing overhead.

  ```
  SELECT customer_id, sales_date, total_amount
  FROM sales;
  ```

- **Use joins effectively.** Prefer inner joins over outer joins when possible and ensure join keys are indexed.

  ```
  SELECT c.customer_name, o.order_id
  FROM customers c
  INNER JOIN orders o ON c.customer_id = o.customer_id;
  ```

- **Create materialized views.** Pre-compute and store results of frequent queries to speed up subsequent access.

  ```
  CREATE MATERIALIZED VIEW sales_summary AS
  SELECT region, SUM(total_amount) AS total_sales
  FROM sales
  GROUP BY region;
  ```

- **Implement the search optimization service** for point queries that require fast lookups in large datasets.

- **Remove unnecessary sorts.**

  The ORDER BY created_at DESC inside filtered_orders does not affect the final result since the main query does not require ordered data.

  Sorting inside a CTE is expensive and unnecessary unless explicitly needed for LIMIT or ROW_NUMBER() operations. Removing it reduces query execution time and computational costs in Snowflake see Figure 10-1.

unnecessary_sort.sql

```
with
filtered_orders as (
  select
      *
  from orders
  where
    status='fulfilled'
    and not test
    and created_at > current_date - 90
  order by created_at desc -- REMOVE THIS UNNECESSARY SORT!
),
line_items as (
  select
      *
  from line_items
  where
    created_at > current_date - 90
)
select
  filtered_orders.order_id,
  line_item.product_id
from filtered_orders
inner join line_items
  on filtered_orders.order_id=line_items.order_id
```

Figure 10-1. *Removing sort*

Choose window functions over self-joins. Without self-join, each row is processed only once. Snowflake applies the window function efficiently over partitions, so the execution is faster. Also, the query is easier to understand see Figure 10-2.

CHAPTER 10 PERFORMANCE OPTIMIZATION AND COST MONITORING

```sql
                    window_function_over_self_join.sql
-- Avoid self-joins
select
    o1.date,
    o1.customer_id,
    sum(o2.order_value) as running_total_order_value
from orders as o1
inner join orders as o2
    on o1.customer_id=o2.customer_id
    and o1.date >= o2.date
group by 1,2

-- Use window functions instead
with
daily_customer_value as (
  select
    date,
    customer_id,
    sum(order_value) as total_order_value
  from orders
)
select
    date,
    customer_id,
    sum(total_order_value)
      over (partition by customer_id order by date) as running_total_order_value
from daily_customer_value
```

Figure 10-2. Window functions instead of self-joins

- **Avoid joins with an OR condition.** Using OR conditions in JOIN clauses can significantly degrade query performance because they prevent efficient indexing and partition pruning, leading to full table scans see Figure 10-3.

avoid_or_in_join_condition.sql

```sql
-- Avoid have an OR statement in the join condition
select
  events.*,
  event_map.description as event_description
from events
left join event_map
  on events.code=event_map.code
  or events.type=event_map.type

-- Instead, join twice
select
  events.*,
  coalesce(event_map_1.description, event_mape_2.description) as event_description
from events
left join event_map as event_map_1
  on events.code=event_map_1.code
left join event_map as event_map_2
  or events.type=event_map_2.type
```

Figure 10-3. *Avoid joins with an OR condition*

- **Periodically review long-running queries** in the Query History dashboard to identify candidates for optimization.

Leverage Caching

Snowflake caches data at multiple levels—result caching, query caching, and warehouse caching—to reduce redundant computation and enhance performance. If a user runs the same query twice within 24 hours and the underlying data has not changed, Snowflake returns the cached result immediately.

Warehouse Configuration Optimization

Right-sizing Virtual Warehouses

Select an appropriate size based on query complexity and concurrency. If a marketing team is running ad hoc reports with minimal concurrency, an XS or S warehouse is cost-effective. For a nightly batch ETL process, a L warehouse may be more efficient.

Scaling Policies

Use auto-scaling to dynamically adjust warehouse clusters based on demand. During business hours, enable auto-scaling to handle spikes in user activity and suspend the warehouse after hours to save costs.

Snowflake has introduced several recent features that can further improve performance and efficiency.

- **Cluster size tuning**: Independent from warehouse size, this allows better management of concurrency. Larger cluster sizes can process more queries in parallel, reducing queue times.

- **Query acceleration service** (QAS): This optional feature uses ephemeral compute resources behind the scenes to speed up large, complex queries—especially useful in dashboards or high-concurrency environments.

- **Snowpark-optimized warehouses**: Designed for memory-intensive operations, these specialized warehouses provide more memory per node and are optimized for workloads using Snowpark (e.g., ML model training or large in-memory data transformations).

By leveraging these architectural features effectively, you can achieve a balance between performance and cost.

Administering Resource Consumption

The next important topic for Snowflake administrators is resource consumption. Keeping track of storage and compute resources is critical for Snowflake customers. Snowflake provides administrative capabilities for monitoring credit and storage usage as well as resource monitors that can send alerts on usage spikes and automatically suspend the virtual warehouse.

By default, only the ACCOUNTADMIN role has access to the billing information. Access to this data can be extended to other roles by granting the appropriate privileges, such as the **MONITOR USAGE** or **MONITOR ACCOUNT** privileges.

Snowflake's unique architecture separates compute resources (virtual warehouses) from data storage. Costs are based on the following.

- **Compute costs**: Measured in credits for the time virtual warehouses run.
- **Storage costs**: Based on the volume of data stored in Snowflake.

When setting up a Snowflake demo account for this book, we were granted 400 credits to use, and Snowflake administrators can track credit consumption in real time.

Virtual Warehouse Usage

Snowflake charges credits for using virtual warehouses (VWs), and the price depends on the number of VWs in use, their size, and usage duration.

Note Credits are billed per second, with a 60-second minimum per usage session.

You can use the WAREHOUSE_METERING_HISTORY table function that shows hourly credit usage, or you can use the web interface and click Admin ➤ Cost Management. Let's run this code to see the usage for the last seven days.

```
select * from table(information_schema.warehouse_metering_history(dateadd('days',-7,current_date()))); 
```

Figure 10-4 shows an example of sample usage.

```
14  select * from table(information_schema.warehouse_metering_history(dateadd('days',-7,current_date())));
15
```

START_TIME	END_TIME	WAREHOUSE_NAME	CREDITS_USED	CREDITS_USED_COMPUTE	CREDITS_USED_CLOUD_SERVICES
2025-01-15 02:00:00.000 -0800	2025-01-15 03:00:00.000 -0800	COMPUTE_WH	0.183867222	0.183333333	0.000533889
2025-01-15 07:00:00.000 -0800	2025-01-15 08:00:00.000 -0800	COMPUTE_WH	0.220118889	0.220000000	0.000118889
2025-01-16 00:00:00.000 -0800	2025-01-16 01:00:00.000 -0800	COMPUTE_WH	0.264108611	0.263333333	0.000775278
2025-01-14 00:00:00.000 -0800	2025-01-14 01:00:00.000 -0800	CLOUD_SERVICES_ONLY	0.000004722	0.000000000	0.000004722
2025-01-15 02:00:00.000 -0800	2025-01-15 03:00:00.000 -0800	CLOUD_SERVICES_ONLY	0.000017500	0.000000000	0.000017500
2025-01-15 07:00:00.000 -0800	2025-01-15 08:00:00.000 -0800	CLOUD_SERVICES_ONLY	0.000023333	0.000000000	0.000023333
2025-01-15 23:00:00.000 -0800	2025-01-16 00:00:00.000 -0800	CLOUD_SERVICES_ONLY	0.000005278	0.000000000	0.000005278
2025-01-16 00:00:00.000 -0800	2025-01-16 01:00:00.000 -0800	CLOUD_SERVICES_ONLY	0.000005278	0.000000000	0.000005278

Figure 10-4. Sample usage of credits for virtual warehouse

Note Use virtual warehouse auto-suspend and auto-resume settings to minimize compute costs.

-- Auto-suspend after 60 seconds of inactivity.

ALTER WAREHOUSE my_warehouse SET AUTO_SUSPEND = 60, AUTO_RESUME = TRUE ;

Data Storage Usage

Another aspect of the price is storage. Snowflake calculates the price of storage monthly based on the average daily storage space. It includes files stored in the Snowflake stage, data stored in databases, and historical data maintained for a fail-safe. Moreover, time-traveling and cloned objects are consuming storage. The price is based on a flat rate per terabyte.

Note The terabyte price depends on the type of account (capacity or on-demand), region, and cloud provider.

You can review the usage data using the web interface, navigating to Admin ➤ Cost Management ➤ Consumption, and selecting **Storage** in the Usage Type menu. The result is shown in Figure 10-5.

CHAPTER 10 PERFORMANCE OPTIMIZATION AND COST MONITORING

Figure 10-5. *Snowflake usage report*

Also, you can leverage table functions and a Snowflake view, as follows.

```
-- Database Storage for last 7 days
select * from table(information_schema.database_storage_usage_history(dateadd('days',-7,current_date()),current_date()));
-- Stage Storage for last 7 days
select * from table(information_schema.stage_storage_usage_history(dateadd('days',-7,current_date()),current_date()));
-- Table Storage utilization
select * from table_storage_metrics
```

Note Make sure that data is in a compressed format in the Snowflake staging area. Another consideration is to use external storage options like Amazon S3, where you can set the data lifecycle policy and archive cold data. Reduce retention periods for non-critical data to minimize storage costs.

```
ALTER TABLE my_table SET DATA_RETENTION_TIME_IN_DAYS = 1;
```

Data Transfer Usage

Snowflake is available in multiple regions for AWS, Azure, and Google Cloud Platform. You should take into consideration one more aspect of possible cost. If you are using an external stage (AWS S3 or Azure Blob Storage), you may be charged for data transfers between regions.

Snowflake charges a fee for unloading data into S3 or Blog Storage within the same region or across regions.

Note Snowflake won't charge you for loading data from external storage.

There is an internal Snowflake function that helps track this cost, as shown here.

```
-- Cost for the last 7 days
select * from table(information_schema.data_transfer_history(date_range_start=>dateadd('day',-7,current_date()),date_range_end=>current_date()));
```

Configure Resource Monitors

Resource monitors allow you to restrict the total cost a given warehouse can incur. You can use resource monitors for two purposes.

- To send a notification once costs reach a certain threshold
- To restrict a warehouse from costing more than a certain amount in a given time period

Snowflake can prevent queries from running on a warehouse if it has surpassed its quota.

Figure 10-6 is a screenshot of the Snowflake resource monitor.

CHAPTER 10   PERFORMANCE OPTIMIZATION AND COST MONITORING

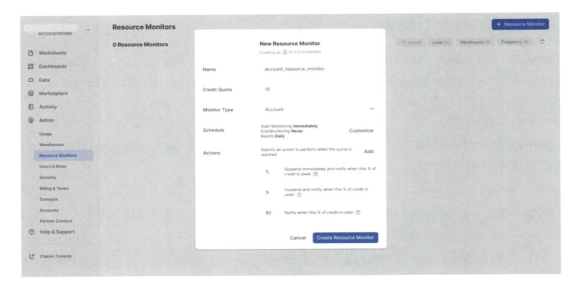

Figure 10-6. Snowflake resource monitor

Resource monitors are a great way to avoid surprises in your bill and prevent unnecessary costs from occurring in the first place.

Configure Budgets

In addition to resource monitors, Snowflake now offers a more advanced feature: Budgets. Budgets provide a broader view of anticipated spending across the account and support more proactive financial planning.

The following are key features of budgets.

- Set spending limits over custom timeframes (monthly, quarterly, etc.)
- Monitor actual vs. forecasted credit consumption
- Receive alerts when spending is projected to exceed the budget
- Track usage across multiple objects, such as warehouses, services, and features

Budgets can be especially helpful for finance and FinOps teams to anticipate overspending before it occurs rather than simply reacting to usage limits.

You can configure Budgets via SQL or the Snowsight UI under Admin ➤ Cost Management ➤ Budgets.

For more information, see the Snowflake Budgets documentation at `https://docs.snowflake.com/en/user-guide/budgets`.

Summary

Optimizing Snowflake isn't just about performance—it's about aligning architecture, workloads, and cost management in a way that scales with your organization's needs. This chapter explored practical strategies across warehouse configuration, query and data optimization, and spend governance. Whether it's fine-tuning clustering keys, enabling auto-scaling, leveraging budgets, or monitoring credit usage, each decision contributes to a more responsive, efficient, and cost-effective data platform.

By applying these best practices, you'll not only improve query speeds and resource utilization but also gain better control over your Snowflake environment—ensuring it delivers value at every level of usage.

CHAPTER 11

Snowflake AI and ML

Data is everywhere, and turning that raw data into real understanding can feel like searching for a needle in a haystack. There are times when we need to uncover the hidden stories, predict what's coming next, or make smart decisions based on solid evidence. But that's all changing with Snowflake ML. You don't need to be a data scientist or have a PhD to get started, putting the power of artificial intelligence and machine learning within reach of anyone, regardless of their background. This chapter covers the following topics.

- Overview and key features
- Data preparation
- Best practices

After completing this chapter, you should have a high-level understanding of how to navigate and use Snowflake ML.

Overview and Key Features

Snowflake ML is a powerful service integrated within the Snowflake AI Data Cloud. It enables users to build, leverage, and maintain machine learning (ML) models. Additionally, Snowflake AI and ML Studio incorporate large language models (LLMs) that enable advanced text generation, summarization, code completion, and other AI-powered tasks directly within Snowflake. You also have access to tools like Document AI, Cortex Playground, Cortex Search, Cortex Analyst, and Snowflake Copilot, which are all part of Snowflake ML.

Chapter 11   SNOWFLAKE AI AND ML

Key Features

This section provides a high-level overview of Snowflake ML's key features, including core capabilities of the pretrained ML and LLM functions, custom model deployment, embeddings, and other services, demonstrating how they work together to empower users of all skill levels.

Pretrained ML Models

Snowflake offers a library of pretrained ML models for common tasks such as classification, anomaly detection, forecasting, and more. These models can be used directly within SQL queries, eliminating the need for complex integrations or additional infrastructure.

Classification

You are asked to predict what type of spender (i.e., high, medium, low) a new customer could become based on what they buy. Snowflake makes it easy with its predefined classification model. To prepare for use, you need to provide a training table with one or more features that correspond to the spend category into which these customers fall. Then, you create another table that applies the model, which contains the same features. Figure 11-1 shows how to get started.

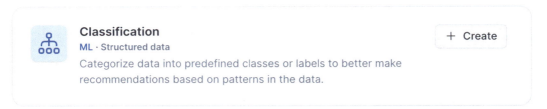

Figure 11-1.   To get started, click + Create Classification ML under the Snowflake AI and ML Studio options

Forecasting

Your finance team needs to forecast monthly revenue, and they'd like to account for variations with holidays and slow periods. Snowflake offers a way to easily create a forecasting ML model. Simply train using your time series data, and the forecast model will provide forecast data. Figure 11-2 shows how to get started.

192

CHAPTER 11 SNOWFLAKE AI AND ML

Figure 11-2. To get started, click + Create Forecasting ML under the Snowflake AI and ML Studio options

Anomaly Detection

You want to be proactive instead of reactive when it comes to discovering data quality issues. An anomaly detection model would help monitor your pipelines and alert you for any outliers or uncommon events that can affect your data quality. To utilize, the training dataset needs a timestamp column and at least one numeric column. Figure 11-3 shows how to get started.

Figure 11-3. Create Anomaly Detection ML under the Snowflake AI and ML Studio options

LLM Functions

Snowflake offers instant and easy access to well-known LLMs from companies like Anthropic and Meta through easy-to-use functions. These functions allow users to leverage the power of LLMs directly within Snowflake without a complicated setup. You can easily perform tasks such as text summarization, sentiment analysis, and language translation directly on data stored in Snowflake tables. For example, a user could use an LLM Function to automatically summarize customer reviews or analyze the sentiment of social media posts related to their brand. Figure 11-4 shows an example of how to use the `SNOWFLAKE.CORTEX.COMPLETE()` function within a simple SQL statement.

CHAPTER 11   SNOWFLAKE AI AND ML

***Figure 11-4.** Simple SQL Statement using the Complete function, one of many Snowflake LLM functions*

For a complete list of LLM functions, please see Snowflake's documentation at `https://docs.snowflake.com/en/user-guide/snowflake-cortex/llm-functions`.

Custom Model Deployment

Users can train and deploy their own ML models within Snowflake using Snowpark ML, which allows the use of Python-based frameworks like TensorFlow, PyTorch, and Scikit-learn. Snowflake has an excellent tutorial on how to deploy a custom model to the Snowflake Model Registry.

Tip   Read the Deploying Custom Models To Snowflake Model Registry tutorial at `https://quickstarts.snowflake.com/guide/deploying_custom_models_to_snowflake_model_registry/index.html#0`.

Embeddings

Snowflake supports vectorized data processing, enabling similarity searches and recommendation systems. This is particularly useful for applications such as image recognition, personalized recommendations, and NLP-based search functions. To use the embeddings vector functions, first store the embeddings in a Snowflake table and then perform the similarity comparisons. The following is an example of how easily you can use embeddings for cosine similarity.

```
SELECT item_id, VECTOR_COSINE_SIMILARITY(embedding_column, input_vector) AS
similarity FROM my_embeddings_table ORDER BY similarity DESC LIMIT 10;
```

Feature Store

Snowflake's Feature Store is a centralized registry for ML features, which are datasets that are preprocessed and used for model inputs. Data preparation is discussed in the next section, with strategies on how to create Snowflake datasets for model training and inputs. But, adding a dataset to the Feature Store is simple. You can run a simple Python command. Please keep in mind that access to these datasets is managed by Snowflake roles.

```
from snowflake.ml.feature_store import FeatureStore, CreationMode

fs = FeatureStore(
      session=session,
      database="MY_DB",
      name="MY_FEATURE_STORE",
      default_warehouse="MY_WH",
      creation_mode=CreationMode.CREATE_IF_NOT_EXIST,
)
```

Note Snowflake Feature Store is an Enterprise Edition product and may require changes to your account. Contact Snowflake support for assistance on upgrading.

See Snowflake's documentation on the Feature Store for more information on role-based access and working with different types of datasets (https://docs.snowflake.com/en/developer-guide/snowflake-ml/feature-store/overview).

CHAPTER 11 SNOWFLAKE AI AND ML

Snowflake Copilot

An LLM assistant that helps users understand their data with natural language queries, generate and refine SQL queries, and learn about Snowflake's features. Figure 11-5 shows how asking a question in Copilot generates a query that you can easily add and/or run within our Snowflake worksheet.

Figure 11-5. Generate a query that you can easily add and/or run within a Snowflake worksheet

> **TRY OUT SNOWFLAKE COPILOT**
>
> 1. Select **Database** and **Schema**. In this example, we selected SNOWFLAKE_SAMPLE_DATA.TPCH_SF
>
> 2. Enter a question you'd like help with. The request in Figure 11-5 is *Help me create a query that shows the number of customers and count orders for each nation.*
>
> 3. Click **Run** to move the query to the Worksheet and run the query at the same time. If you only want to move the query to the Worksheet without running, click **+Add**.

Document AI

This feature intelligently processes and extracts structured data from unstructured content like PDFs, images, and Word files at scale, simplifying document handling. This is a very useful tool, and Snowflake offers a very useful tutorial on their site.

> **Tip** Create a document processing pipeline with Document AI. To start this tutorial, visit https://docs.snowflake.com/en/user-guide/snowflake-cortex/document-ai/tutorials/create-processing-pipelines

Cortex Search

A text search service that provides LLMs with context from your latest proprietary data, enabling more accurate and relevant results. Snowflake offers an easy walk-through guide the first time it is used. This guide can be started in the Snowflake AI and ML Studio.

CHAPTER 11 SNOWFLAKE AI AND ML

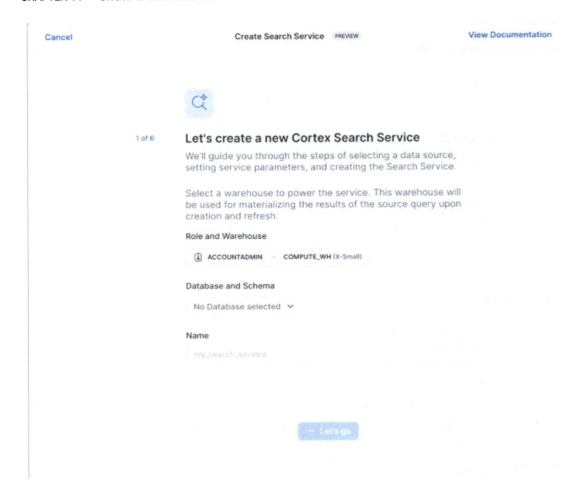

Figure 11-6. First screen of the Cortex Search tutorial, located in the Snowflake AI and ML Studio

Cortex Analyst

Create an LLM-powered application using your business terms along with your data. This helps users ask questions as they would to an analyst—naturally and conversationally. The application would generate the necessary queries in the background and present the answers without the user having to write code or create dashboards. This helps scale your analytics team to work on more complex problems.

To try it out, Snowflake integrates a tutorial in the Snowflake AI and ML Studio. Find **Cortex Analyst**, click **Try,** and then click **+ Create new** (see Figure 11-7).

CHAPTER 11 SNOWFLAKE AI AND ML

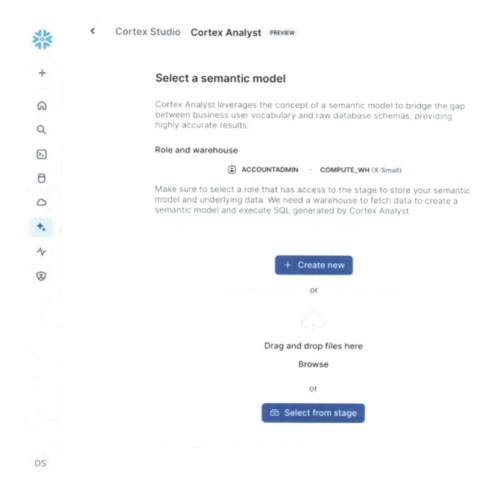

Figure 11-7. Cortex Analyst screen: to begin tutorial walk-through, click + Create New

Without high-quality, well-prepared data, even the most sophisticated models struggle to produce meaningful results. Snowflake, with its robust data management capabilities, provides an ideal environment for preparing data for generative AI projects. This section delves into the essential steps involved in this process, from data discovery to ensuring data governance and security. Utilizing Snowflakes features for data discovery and transformation techniques for data cleaning that help improve your data quality is also covered.

Data Discovery

Data discovery is crucial for any AI project, as it helps identify relevant data sources and their characteristics and ensures that the project starts with a solid foundation of suitable data. Snowflake offers data profiling SQL commands and tagging as a way to facilitate your data discovery.

Snowflake has built-in SQL commands that allow you to quickly analyze the characteristics of your data. This includes identifying data types, distributions, null values, and other statistical properties. This information is crucial for understanding the data's suitability for most AI projects while also identifying potential data quality issues. You can use SQL commands like DESCRIBE TABLE, SHOW TABLES, and INFORMATION_SCHEMA views to gain insights into your data.

The following shows how to get useful metadata about your tables from the INFORMATION_SCHEMA table.

```
SELECT column_name, data_type, null_count, distinct_count
FROM information_schema.columns
WHERE table_name = 'my_table';
```

Snowflake also allows you to tag data objects (i.e., tables, views, columns) with metadata. This enables you to organize and categorize your data, making it easier to discover relevant datasets. For example, you might tag a table containing customer reviews with "sentiment analysis" or a dataset of images with "image generation."

The following is an example of how to add a tag to a table named customer_reviews.

```
ALTER TABLE customer_reviews SET TAG data_domain = 'customer_feedback';
```

By effectively using the data profiling SQL commands and tagging your datasets, you can quickly and efficiently identify and select the relevant data for your project.

Data Cleaning and Transformation

Once you've identified suitable datasets, the next step is to clean and transform the data to make it suitable for use in AI projects. This often involves addressing several common data quality issues, which are missing values (nulls vs. blanks), irrelevant data, outlier detection and treatment, data type conversion, and more. There are entire books written on just this subject, but this book covers some ways you can clean your data with Snowflakes SQL functions or commands.

Handling Missing Values

Missing data can significantly impact model performance. The best method for handling missing values depends on several factors, including the amount of missing data, the type of data, and the impact of missing data. Snowflake provides functions that make it easy to handle missing values, including the following.

- **Removing**: Removing an entire row where any value is missing is the easiest to implement but may also reduce the number of rows. This can be done by filtering using the WHERE clause.

- **Imputation**: Replacing missing values with another value, such as estimated values (e.g., mean, median, mode) or replacing NULL or blanks with zero. This can be done using SQL's COALESCE or NVL functions.

Outlier Detection and Treatment

Outliers can skew and lead to inaccurate or unintentional results. Snowflake offers many statistical functions that can be used to detect outliers, such as STDDEV(), STDDEV_SAMP(), STDDEV_POP(), PERCENTILE_CONT(), and APPROX_PERCENTILE().

Data Type Conversion

LLM prompts are in text format, which may require converting data in your table to text. Snowflake has SQL functions like CAST and TO_VARCHAR that dynamically convert your non-text data into text.

Best Practices for Using Snowflake ML

- **Optimize data storage**: Store only relevant features for ML models to reduce costs and improve query performance. For example, instead of storing entire raw datasets, extract key attributes such as transaction amounts and timestamps for fraud detection models.

- **Monitor model performance**: Regularly evaluate the performance of deployed models and update them as needed. This can be done by comparing model predictions against actual outcomes, such as tracking the accuracy of a customer churn prediction model over time.

- **Workflow automation**: Automate AI/ML pipelines using workflow tools like Snowpark or Airflow. For instance, businesses can set up automated workflows to retrain fraud detection models daily using the latest transaction data.

- **Caching**: Take advantage of Snowflake's caching mechanisms to speed up AI/ML queries. For example, frequently queried embeddings for recommendation systems can be cached to improve performance and reduce computational costs. One way to cache embeddings is by storing them in a dedicated Snowflake table with optimized indexing and clustering. Additionally, materialized views or temporary tables can be used to cache commonly accessed embeddings, ensuring quick retrieval without recomputing them repeatedly. This approach is particularly useful in applications like real-time recommendation engines, where minimizing latency is critical.

Summary

The knowledge gained from this chapter sets the foundation for integrating machine learning into your workflows and driving meaningful outcomes for your organization. Whether you are exploring pretrained models, preparing data for analysis, or implementing best practices, Snowflake ML provides the tools and flexibility needed to succeed. By combining powerful AI capabilities with the simplicity and scalability of the Snowflake platform, it empowers users to derive actionable insights and make data-driven decisions with ease.

CHAPTER 12

Migrating to Snowflake

Throughout the book, you have learned Snowflake's key concepts, including its architecture and its security capabilities. You have also met some unique Snowflake features. Moreover, you saw how Snowflake can be integrated with third-party tools for ELT/ETL and business intelligence purposes, as well as big data and advanced analytics use cases with Spark.

This chapter highlights some key migration scenarios to give you an idea of how you can migrate your legacy solution to the cloud. In addition, some organizations may attempt to upgrade an existing cloud solution that is insufficient for a business use case or is too expensive.

Data warehouse modernization is a hot topic right now, and many organizations are seeking best practices to modernize their legacy, expensive, and ineffective solutions using the cloud. Snowflake is a good choice for organizations because it is available on major cloud platforms, including Amazon Web Services (AWS), Microsoft Azure, and Google Cloud Platform (GCP), and it enables you to achieve instant value by democratizing data across the organization.

This chapter covers the following topics.

- Data warehouse migration scenarios
- Common data architectures
- Key steps for a data warehouse migration
- Real-world project
- Additional resources for Snowflake migration

CHAPTER 12 MIGRATING TO SNOWFLAKE

Data Warehouse Migration Scenarios

The goal of a data warehouse migration is to serve the growing data appetite of end users who are hungry for data insights. Before diving deep into this topic, let's categorize the organizations and their data needs. We split organizations by their analytics maturity, as shown here.

- Startups and small businesses without a proper analytics solution
- Organizations with on-premise data solutions
- Organizations with a default cloud solution deployed on Azure, GCP, or AWS

Startup or Small Business Analytics Scenario

The easiest deployment process is for startup companies. They don't have any analytics solution yet and are usually connecting to source systems using business intelligence (BI) tools or spreadsheets. They are looking for better alternatives, and they don't want to invest in an expensive solution, but they want to be sure that they can start small and scale easily. With Snowflake, they get all the benefits of Snowflake and pay only for their workloads. Over time, they grow, and as a result, their Snowflake implementation grows.

Figure 12-1 shows an example architecture before Snowflake and with it for small companies.

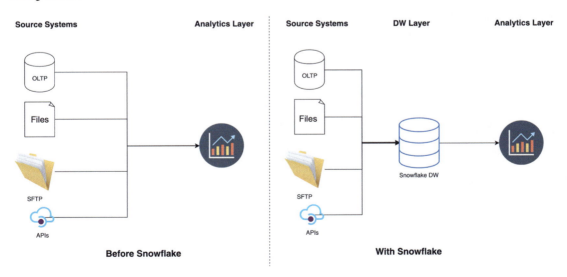

Figure 12-1. Before and with Snowflake for startups

Startups track key metrics, and it is important to get timely insights from data. As a result, analysts connect to the source systems and extract the data. This process is manual and not scalable. The next logical step is to hire a data engineer or analytics consulting company and deploy a data warehouse with Snowflake. This allows you to get insights into your data and grow the business.

On-Premise Analytics Scenario for Enterprises and Large Organizations

The second scenario is the biggest and the most popular. There are lots of enterprise organizations that are looking for a way to improve their existing on-premise solutions. These solutions are extremely expensive, and they require lots of resources to maintain. Moreover, they have lots of custom solutions for big data, streaming, and so on. The complexity of these solutions is extremely high, but the value isn't high because on-premise solutions are a bottleneck, and it is not easy to scale a solution, even in the case of an unlimited budget. So, the best way is to migrate the existing on-premise solutions to the cloud and leverage an innovative analytics data platform such as Snowflake. With Snowflake, enterprises can migrate all their data to the cloud, use a single platform for a data warehouse, share data, and make use of machine learning.

Figure 12-2 shows an example architecture before and with Snowflake for enterprises and other large companies.

CHAPTER 12 MIGRATING TO SNOWFLAKE

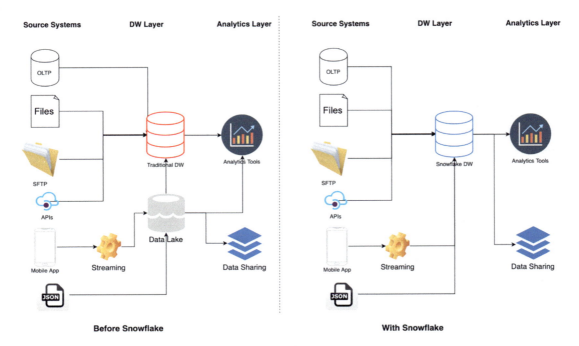

Figure 12-2. Before and with Snowflake for enterprises

The figure is a top-level overview of an on-premise organization with big data (a data lake, usually deployed on top of Hadoop) and an on-premise data warehouse massively parallel processing (MPP) solution such as Oracle, Teradata, or Netezza. Usually, enterprises use enterprise-grade ETL solutions that are expensive and require powerful hardware. There are multiple options for streaming, and one of the most popular is Apache Kafka. Moreover, enterprises handle a large volume of data with a semi-structured format such as JSON, AVRO, Parquet, and so on. Figure 12-2 spotlights uploading JSON into a data lake and then parsing and loading it into a data warehouse. Finally, some organizations have to share data. This isn't an easy or cheap task for an on-premise solution.

With Snowflake, organizations migrate all their data into the cloud. Moreover, they use a single data platform for streaming use cases, storing semi-structured data, and querying the data via SQL without physically moving the data. So, there are lots of benefits that open new horizons for analytics and help to make business decisions driven by data.

CHAPTER 12 MIGRATING TO SNOWFLAKE

Cloud Analytics Modernization with Snowflake

The last scenario is the trickiest one. Some modern organizations have already leveraged cloud vendors or migrated a legacy solution to the cloud. However, they may be facing challenges such as high cost, performance issues related to concurrency, or having multiple tools for various business scenarios such as streaming and big data analytics. As a result, they decide to try Snowflake and unify their data analytics with a single platform and get almost unlimited scalability and elasticity.

Figure 12-3 shows an example architecture before and with Snowflake for cloud deployments with Microsoft Azure.

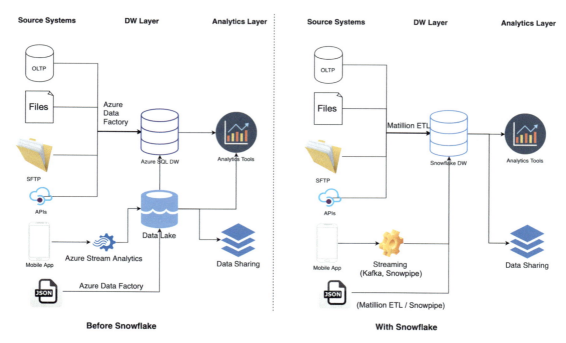

Figure 12-3. *Before and with Snowflake for cloud analytics modernization on Microsoft Azure*

On the left, there are multiple solutions from Azure for the data warehouse and data lake, such as Azure Data Factory and Azure Streaming. On the right, there is Snowflake, which is hosted on the Azure cloud, and we have leveraged another cloud ELT tool, Matillion ETL, that allows you to create complex transformations visually. However, we can still use Azure Data Factory for ELT. Finally, with this new architecture, you can leverage the data sharing capabilities without physically moving the data.

207

Data Warehouse Migration Process

You just reviewed three common scenarios for Snowflake migrations. Let's dive deep into the second scenario because it is one of the most popular and complex. The first scenario isn't a real migration scenario; it is more a data warehouse design and implementation project. The third scenario is an evolution of the second; it has a similar idea, and usually, it is easier to perform since all the data is already in the cloud.

When we talk about data warehouse migration, there are two major approaches.

- **Lift and shift**: Copy the data as is with limited changes.

- **Split and flip**: Split a solution into logical functional data layers. Match the data functionality with the right technology. Leverage the wide selection of tools on the cloud to best fit the needs. Move data in phases such as prototype, learn, and perfect.

Despite the fact that "lift and shift" is a faster approach, it has limited value for long-term organizational goals. As a result, we always prefer to "split and flip." This guarantees that we won't sacrifice for short-term value.

The migration process can be split into two main buckets.

- The organizational part of the migration project

- The technical part of the migration project

Let's review them in detail.

Organizational Part of the Migration Project

Figure 12-4 shows a high-level overview of the steps needed to prepare and execute the migration of an existing system to Snowflake.

CHAPTER 12 MIGRATING TO SNOWFLAKE

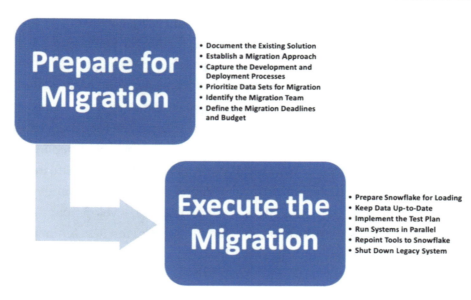

Figure 12-4. *Key steps of the migration process*

Let's learn more about each of the migration steps that are recommended by Snowflake.

Document the Existing Solution

You already know that Snowflake uses role-based access control; therefore, you must document the existing users, their roles, and their permissions. This allows you to replicate the data access and security strategy implemented in your legacy system. You should pay special attention to sensitive datasets and how they're secured, as well as how frequently security provisioning processes run to create similar security within Snowflake. Finally, you want to ensure that you have an existing architectural diagram of the existing solution.

Establish a Migration Approach

Then, you should establish a migration approach. You should list all the existing processes that you want to migrate. Moreover, you should identify all the processes that have to be refactored as well as the broken processes that need to be fixed. This allows you to draft these deliverables and create the data architecture diagram to present to the stakeholders.

Snowflake generally recommends minimal re-engineering for the first iteration unless the current system is truly outdated. To provide value for the business as soon as possible, you should avoid a single "big-bang" deliverable as the migration approach and instead break the migration into incremental deliverables that enable your organization to start making the transition to Snowflake more quickly. This process is called *agile data warehousing* and allows you to deliver fast value for the end users.

Moreover, organizations may want to change their development or deployment processes as part of the migration. You should document new tools that are introduced as a result of the migration, tools that need to be deprecated, and development environments that are needed for the migration. Whether the development and deployment processes change or not, you should capture the development environments that are used for the migration.

Capture the Development and Deployment Processes

Modern organizations care about DevOps. If you haven't widely used it before, it could be a good opportunity to start implementing DevOps/DataOps procedures that increase the quality of your analytics solution; for example, organizations usually have dev, QA, and prod environments.

Moreover, they have source control repositories and methods for capturing deployment changes from one environment to another. These are used for that migration. This information is critical to direct how the development and deployments are implemented.

The ideal candidates for starting the migration provide value to the business and require minimal migration effort.

Prioritize Datasets for Migration

You should learn more about the available datasets in the legacy solutions. Rather than starting with the most complex datasets, we prefer to begin with a simple dataset that can be migrated quickly to establish a foundation through the development and deployment processes that can be reused for the rest of the migration effort. To prioritize datasets for migration, you should understand the dependencies among datasets. Those dependencies need to be documented and conform with business stakeholders. Ideally, this documentation can be captured using an automated process that collects information from existing ETL jobs, job schedules, and so on. This helps you avoid manual work for identifying and documenting changes.

Creating an automated process provides value throughout the migration project by more easily identifying the ongoing changes that occur, as the underlying systems are unlikely to remain static during the migration.

Identify the Migration Team

Another important aspect is building the migration team. Some common roles required for the migration include developer, quality assurance, business owner, project manager, program manager, scrum master, and communication. When a Snowflake solution partner is engaged for migration, they may fulfill multiple needs, including solution design, gathering requirements, delivering migration projects, producing documentation, and conducting Snowflake training.

Based on our experience, the challenge is to change the paradigm from a traditional data warehouse to a cloud data warehouse. Engineers should be prepared to learn new skills and may consider enrolling in additional professional courses related to cloud foundations and Snowflake best practices.

Define the Migration Deadlines and Budget

The expectations for any migration should be clear to all parties. However, the expectations need to be combined with other information that has been gathered to determine whether the deadlines can be met. One of the benefits of gathering all of this information is to establish and communicate achievable deadlines, even if the deadlines are different from what the business expects.

It is common in migration projects that deadlines are defined before evaluating the scope of the project to determine whether the deadlines are achievable, especially if the business is trying to deprecate the legacy system before the renewal date. In situations where the deadline can't be moved, and the migration scope requires more time than is available before the deadline, work needs to be done with the business to agree on a path forward.

Understanding the budget that has been advocated to complete the migration is also critically important. The amount of migration work and the cost associated with the migration work both need to be compared to the available budget to ensure that there are sufficient funds to complete the work. Pausing in the middle of a migration or stopping it altogether is a bad outcome for all involved parties.

When planning the budget, you should estimate the cost of Snowflake deployment and the cost of the migration project.

Determine the Migration Outcomes

Migration outcomes should be used to validate that the migration project is providing the overall benefit the business expects to achieve from the migration. For example, turning off the Oracle database system is one of the desired outcomes. That outcome should be achieved with the migration plan. This documentation can be expressed as success or failure criteria for the migration project and may also include benchmarks that compare process execution. Once compiled, this information should be used for communicating with stakeholders.

After identifying the migration outcomes, you should present them to the business along with the mitigation strategy and confirm the proposed approach meets their requirements. This should be done to set appropriate expectations from the beginning of the migration.

The escalation process needs to be documented, including who is responsible for working on the issue, who is responsible for communicating the progress of the issue, and a list of contexts from the business, Snowflake, and any other involved parties that are involved in resolving the issue.

Establish Security

Depending on the security requirements, there may be a need to capture role creation, user creation, and the granting of users to roles for auditing purposes. While the existing database security can be a good starting point for setting up security within Snowflake, the security model should be evaluated to determine whether there are roles and users who are no longer needed or should be implemented differently as part of the migration to Snowflake. Additional roles may be required to restrict access to sensitive data. Moreover, you can think about improving the solution security by implementing two-step authentication, collecting security logs, and so on.

Develop a Test Plan

Develop a test plan by identifying the appropriate level and scope for each environment. For example, schedules aren't executed in dev but only in QA and prod. Automate as much as possible to ensure repeatable test processes with consistent output for validation purposes and to find agreed-on document acceptance criteria.

Moreover, you should involve business users in this process; they are subject-matter experts and help to evaluate solutions and help you quickly identify the data discrepancies and processes that are wrong.

Prepare Snowflake for Loading

Despite the fact that Snowflake is a SQL data warehouse, it is different from other analytical data warehouse platforms.

When you have physical servers, you can use a dedicated server for each environment (dev, test, prod). The following shows the hierarchy for the on-premise solution.

- Physical server
  - Databases
    - Schemas
      - Tables/views/functions

In the case of Snowflake, you don't have a physical machine. When you sign up for Snowflake, you get the link `https://<our company name>.snowflakecomputing.com/`, and you stick to this account. As a result, you don't have a physical server layer, and you should think about the organization of environments. To solve this particular issue, you have several options.

- Use multiple accounts (different URLs).

- Create many databases with an environment prefix (FIN_DEV, SALES_DEV, FIND_TEST, etc.).

- Create databases that represent your environments, and then create a schema that represents a database.

This requires you to modify data definition language (DDL) while you are moving the schema from the on-premise solution to the cloud. This is one of the biggest engineering efforts in migration. There are a number of tools available for this purpose that can do forward and reverse engineering. Moreover, you can leverage the Snowflake community and learn how others performed this step.

Finally, you should assign databases, database objects, and virtual warehouses to the appropriate security roles.

When you are ready, you can begin loading your initial data into your data warehouse. Many options are available for loading. For example, you can unload data into the cloud storage, such as S3, in the case of using AWS, and then collect this data via Snowflake. Alternatively, you can leverage cloud ETL tools such as AWS Glue (an AWS product) or Matillion ETL (a third-party commercial product). You can even use open source solutions like Apache Airflow or even Python.

Keep Up-to-Date Data (Executing the Migration)

After an initial load of data is complete, you should start to develop incremental load processes. This is the time when ETL/ELT tools are handy and help you to accelerate your development effort.

These processes should be scheduled and take into consideration the appropriate process dependency. The state of the data loading should be clearly understood and communicated. For example, loading is in progress, loading is completed successfully, and load failures occur that need to be addressed. Finally, begin comparing execution timings to ensure that SLAs are being met.

One of the key things is to constantly communicate with business users and allow them to visually track the load process. You can ensure this by collecting ETL logs on all stages of the ETL process and visualizing them with a BI tool.

Implement the Test Plan (Executing the Migration)

Once an ETL/ELT process is in place, testing can begin. You can start with initial data comparisons. This allows you to quickly identify discrepancies and share these results with stakeholders. Additional groups should be engaged after the initial testing is completed. This helps to validate the data and fix issues within a new solution.

Run Systems in Parallel (Executing the Migration)

As business units are engaged in testing, you should run both systems (the legacy data warehouse and the Snowflake data warehouse) in parallel to ensure the continued validation of data to facilitate comparing data. In some cases, you may export data from a legacy data warehouse, which can be used for comparing data at the raw level. These comparisons should take place in Snowflake, where resources can be provisioned to compare data without negatively impacting the system.

You should attempt to minimize the time the two systems are running in parallel while still maintaining a sufficient validation process.

Repoint Tools to Snowflake

Up until now, the migration process has been focused on raw data comparisons. The final step is to point all business users' connections to the new Snowflake data warehouse. After the business units have validated that their tools are producing the required results, they cut over to Snowflake, begin scheduling, and communicate the cutover plans to all stakeholders.

Once the cutover is complete, users should have the ability to log in to BI tools and repoint them to the Snowflake data warehouse.

Technical Aspects of a Migration Project

Figure 12-5 shows the key elements of a migration project from a technical point of view for a traditional on-premise data warehouse.

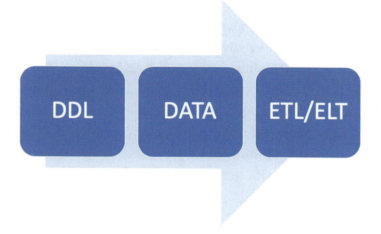

Figure 12-5. Simplified data warehouse migration flow

Let's consider an example where we have an on-premise data warehouse to move to Snowflake. We should start with the DDL for moving the schemas, tables, views, and so on. There are many ways to replicate a data warehouse model in Snowflake, starting from the Python scripts that convert the source system's DDL into Snowflake DDL. In addition, we can leverage data modeling tools like SqlDBM that have good integration with Snowflake and can copy the source system DDL, convert it to Snowflake DDL, and deploy it into Snowflake. Moreover, we can use other tools that support forward and reverse engineering. This helps automate this process and saves time and money.

After the DDL, we should move data. There are many approaches to do this. We can leverage cloud ETL tool capabilities and migrate data from an on-premise solution to Snowflake. For example, Matillion ETL can connect to the on-premise data warehouse and load data directly to Snowflake using cloud data storage such as S3, Blob Storage, and so on. This is an efficient way of moving data. Or, you could leverage Snowflake's SnowSQL CLI and load data with the help of SQL. It is totally up to you. In some extreme cases, for a large volume of data, you might use physical devices such as AWS Snowball or Azure Data Box.

Finally, the most complicated part is migrating the ETL/ELT logic. This is the longest part, and there is a linear correlation between the number of data warehouse objects and the time it takes to perform a migration. This is the time to decide whether you want to migrate existing logic as is (lift and shift) or to work closely with the business stakeholders and learn about the business logic behind the code so you can take it apart and improve it (split and flip).

From a tools standpoint, you can leverage scripting in Python, or you can leverage Snowflake Partner Connect and choose an ETL tool that was built specifically for the Snowflake data warehouse. Some tools are managed services, and others give you more freedom. For example, Matillion provides a virtual machine that is hosted in our virtual private cloud (VPC), and you can establish a mature security level. Moreover, when using ETL tools, you can create a pattern and then copy this pattern across the use cases. The tools also allow end users to follow the process and visually observe the data flow. Finally, Snowflake supports stored procedures, and this gives you the ability to implement an ETL solution with stored procedures like previously done in Oracle, Teradata, or SQL Server.

Real-World Migration Project

Let's look at a real-world project. Figure 12-6 shows an architecture diagram for an e-commerce company that is selling used books online.

CHAPTER 12 MIGRATING TO SNOWFLAKE

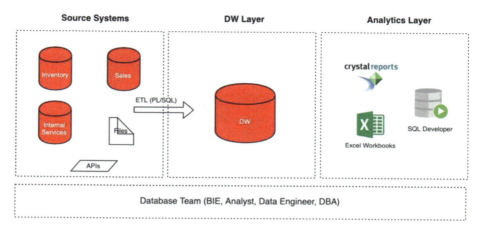

Figure 12-6. Legacy data warehouse architecture

It is a straightforward solution that was built on an Oracle database technology stack. It used PL/SQL as a main ETL tool, and with daily ETL, it was loading data from several transactional systems as well as consuming data from marketing-specific APIs and secure file transfer protocols (SFTPs). These were the challenges.

- The solution was expensive from a licensing perspective.

- ETL was complicated, and the database team owned the logic. They were a kind of bottleneck for all new requests.

- The data warehouse had storage and compute limitations.

- The data warehouse required full-time DBA support (for patching, backups, and so on).

- Performance was an issue and required deep knowledge of Oracle sizing and tuning (indexes, keys, partitions, query plans, and so on).

The company decided to move to the cloud to get more room to grow and to get the benefits of a cloud infrastructure. Figure 12-7 shows an architecture diagram of the new solution. This organization decided to go with Snowflake because it wanted to have unlimited concurrency for queries, a consolidated data warehouse, and a big data solution on a single data platform, as well as dedicated virtual warehouses for analysts with heavy queries.

CHAPTER 12 MIGRATING TO SNOWFLAKE

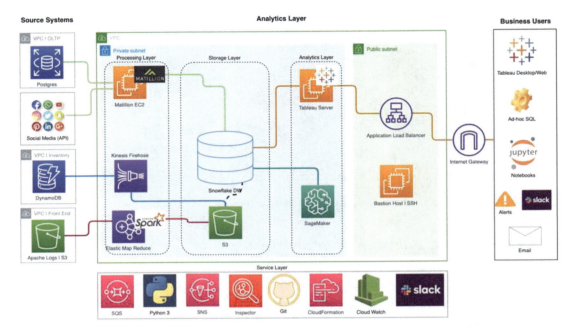

Figure 12-7. Modern data warehouse architecture with Snowflake

Another major decision was made regarding the ETL tool. We reviewed several tools and decided to go with Matillion ETL because it was built specifically for Snowflake and allows you to solve previous challenges with "bottlenecks" in the ETL process. It has an intuitive user interface and doesn't require any coding knowledge. In addition, the organization deployed Tableau as its primary BI tool and adopted self-service analytics; that's why concurrency is a significant benefit of Snowflake. Moreover, the choice addressed another security requirement because it deploys within a private subnet in AWS VPC.

Snowflake helps leverage big data and streaming capabilities that were impossible with the legacy solution. For big data, we were processing web logs within Apache Spark deployed on top of the Amazon Elastic MapReduce (EMR), cluster. Snowflake accesses Parquet files, and we don't need to load them into Snowflake. For the streaming use case, we leveraged DynamoDB streams and Kinesis Firehose, and all data is sent into an S3 bucket where Snowflake can consume it.

This core project with an Oracle data warehouse and ETL migration took us six months with a team of two engineers; it took another three to four months to design and implement the streaming and big data solutions. The organization also leveraged the AWS SageMaker service for machine learning and advanced analytics, which can be easily connected to Snowflake to query data from Snowflake and write model results back to it.

Additional Resources

Working with Snowflake requires you to have a new set of skills related to cloud computing. If you want to succeed with Snowflake, you should learn the best practices for deploying cloud analytics solutions and follow the market trends by reviewing new tools and methods for data processing and transformation in the cloud.

Currently, Snowflake is available in AWS, Microsoft Azure, and GCP. We highly recommend you study a cloud vendor's learning materials to get a better understanding of cloud computing and data storage. For example, if you deploy Snowflake using AWS, you may start with the AWS Technical Essentials course, which is free and gives you an overview of AWS. Then, you can go deeper with AWS analytics using big data specialization.

At the same time, you should learn Snowflake best practices using Snowflake training resources, community websites, and blog posts. This book is a good start.

Summary

This chapter discussed the needs of organizations based on their maturity model and identified three common organizational types. Then, you learned about the legacy data warehouse modernization process and identified the key steps. Finally, you examined a real-world project of migrating to Snowflake and gained insight into its data architecture and project outcomes.

Index

A

Access control models, 60
ACCOUNTADMIN role, 61, 68, 73
<accountname>-snowpipebucket, 46
ACID, *see* Atomicity, consistency, isolation, durability (ACID)
Agile data warehousing, 210
Airbyte, 160, 169
Amazon Redshift, 5, 6, 10
Anomaly detection model, 193
Apache Airflow, 160, 214
Apache Iceberg, 119
    actual data files, 129
    benefits, 119
    catalog, 120
    integration, 121, 122
    key layers, 120
    metadata files, 128
    table
        ARN, 125
        AWS console, 123
        AWS IAM policy, 123–125
        AWS IAM role, 125
        creation, 122
        external computing, 129–131
        external volumes, 123, 126
        IAM user permissions, 126
        ingest data, 128
        queries, 128
        SnowSight, 123
        SQL, 127
        trust relationships, 126, 127
        virtual environment, 122
Atomicity, consistency, isolation, durability (ACID), 4, 5
AWS Kinesis, 42
AWS Lambda, 53
AWS Managed Streaming service for Kafka, 42
AWS Snowball, 216
Azure Data Box, 216

B

Big data, 3, 4, 6, 13
BI tool, 149, 204
Budgets, 188, 189
Bulk data loading, 28, 29
Business intelligence (BI), 1, 4, 6

C

Cache embeddings, 202
Cloud computing, 1, 6
    cloud deployment models, 9
    cloud service models, 9, 10
    definition, 6
    hypervisors, 7, 8
    key elements, 6, 7
    key terms, 7
    migration, 12
    SRM, 11
    virtualization, 8

INDEX

Cloud providers, 12
Cloud resources, 11
Cloud service models, 9, 10
Cloud software distribution model, 10
Cloud technologies, 1
CloudWatch logging, 51
CloudWatch service, 51
Compression methods, 29
COPY command, 39, 41, 44
Cortex Analyst screen, 199
CREATE WAREHOUSE command, 56

D

DAC, *see* Discretionary access control (DAC)
Databricks, 6, 118, 147
Data clustering, 80
Data clustering and partitioning, 175–177
Data discovery, 199, 200
Data lakes, 4, 6, 206, 207
Data loading methods, 28
    bulk loading, 28
    compression methods, 29
    CSV file preparation, 32
    encryption options, 30
    file formats, 30
    file sizing, 31
    file staging, 33, 34
    loading data files, 34
    semi-structured data, 32, 33
Data platform vendors, 119
Data processing optimization
    clustered data., 178
    execution plans, 178
    tools and techniques, 178
DATA_SCIENCE_TEAM role, 65, 67, 68, 70

Data sharing, 85
    secure view, 97
        best practice, 93
        consumer account, 97, 98
        current_account() function, 96
        data, 96
        mapping table, 95
        share object, 97
        sharing table, 94
        test access, 96
Data warehouse as a service (DWaaS), 10–12
Data warehouse loading approaches, 40
Data warehouse migration
    architecture, 204
    business analytics, 204
    cloud analytics, 207
    DW migration, 208
    goal, 204
    on-premise analytics, 205, 206
    organizational part
        data, 214
        data sets, 210
        deadlines/budget, 211
        development/deployment process, 210
        documentation, 209
        migration approach, 209
        migration team, 211
        outcomes, 212
        repoint tools, 215
        run, 214, 215
        security, 212
        Snowflake, 213
        test plan, 212, 214
    overview, 208, 209
    technicalpart, 215, 216
Data warehouses, 3–6, 38, 39
dbt code and modules, 167

INDEX

dbt Core, 159, 161, 162
Discretionary access control (DAC), 60
DWaaS, *see* Data warehouse as a service (DWaaS)
Dynamic data masking, 60, 71–74
Dynamic tables, 54
    automatic refresh, 55
    feature, 54
    JSON data, 58
    scalability, 55
    steps to create, 55, 56

E

Encryption, 30, 72
ETL/ELT logic, 216
ETL/ELT tools, 214
ETL tools, 216
Extract-load-transform (ELT), 2
Extract-transform-load (ETL), 86

F

File formats, 28, 30, 79, 119, 121
Forecasting ML model, 192
Forecast model, 192
Fraud detection models, 201

G

GitHub Codespaces, 162
GitHub repo, 161, 166
Google Cloud Platform, 12
GreenWave Technologies, 152

H

Hadoop, 3, 4, 6, 206
Hosted Apache Kafka, 42

I, J

Identity and Access Management (IAM), 123–126

K

kubectl, 169, 170
Kubernetes clusters, 159, 161, 169–171

L

Lake house, 6
Large language models (LLMs), 191–194, 201
LLM assistant, 196
LLM function, 192–194

M, N

Machine learning (ML), 191, 205
Manual clustering, 176
Marketing role, 60, 61
MARKETING_TEAM role, 65, 66, 68, 70
Massively parallel processing (MPP), 2–5, 11, 13, 206
Materialized views, 81–82, 98–99, 202
Matillion box, 150
Matillion ETL, 149–151, 153, 155, 216
Matillion Objects, 150
Matillion web interface, 151, 152
Metabase, 160, 165–167
Missing data, 142, 143, 201
ML, *see* Machine learning (ML)
Modern analytics solution architecture, 146, 147, 151
Modern solution architecture, 118, 119
    AWS IAM policy, 124, 125
    AWS IAM role, 125, 126

223

INDEX

Modern solution architecture (*cont.*)
    Iceberg actual data files, S3, 129
    Iceberg data files, S3, 129
    key elements, 118, 119
    options, 121
Monitor performance, 177
MPP, *see* Massively parallel processing (MPP)

O

Optimization techniques, 175
    datasets, 179
    unnecessary data, 178
Oracle, 3, 5, 206, 212, 216–218
Outliers, 193, 200, 201

P, Q

Partition pruning, 80, 175
Partner Connect, 148, 150, 216
Permifrost, 68–71
Personally Identifiable Information (PII), 71, 72
Pre-Commit Hooks, 168
Predefined classification model, 192
Proof of concept (PoC), 159
Public clouds, 9, 159
Python command, 195

R

Real-world project
    big data, 218
    challenges, 217
    ETL tool, 218
    legacy DW architecture, 216, 217
    modern DW architecture, 217, 218
    streaming, 218
    Tableau, 218
Resource monitors, 184, 187, 188
Role-based access control (RBAC), 60
    best practices, 68
    Permifrost, 68–71
    working with roles and users, 65–68
R/Python scripts, 3

S

Securable objects, 60
Secure data sharing, 72, 79, 85–99
SECURITYADMIN role, 61, 65
Semi-structured data, 18, 32–33, 41, 82
Shared responsibility model (SRM), 11
SMP, *see* Symmetric multiprocessing (SMP)
Snowflake, 10, 146, 148, 150, 154, 158, 159, 171, 174–177, 179, 180, 182–189, 191–194, 197–201, 205
    architectural features
        automatic query optimization, 174
        cloud-based storage, 174
        warehouses, 174
    architecture, 13
    cloud providers, 12
    cloud storage and computing, 14
    competitors, 11
    data sharing
        advantages, 87
        benefits, 86
        database objects, 87
        process, 87–89
        provider and consumer, 87
    dbt Core, 162
    dbt project, 163, 164
    drivers, 149

INDEX

environment, 189
ETL process, 14
features, 13, 15
key layers, 14
Matillion, 148, 150
pain points, data warehouse, 6
regular *vs.* materialized views, 98, 99
role, 145
and SMP/MPP architectures, 13
table sharing
    consumer account, 92, 93
    creation, 90
    grants, 92
    metadata, 92
    results, 93
    steps, 89
    stock data, 91
teams/departments, 14
and traditional data warehouse, 12
views, 165
worksheet, 196
Snowflake account, 18
    cloud providers and regions, 19, 20
    editions, 19
    pricing model, 20
Snowflake administration
    account parameters, 77, 78
    commands, manage users, 65
    commands, role management, 65
    custom role hierarchy, 61, 62
    database objects, 78, 79
    data shares, 79, 80
    manage warehouses, 73, 74
    managing databases, 74, 75
    MARKETING_TEAM role, 66
    materialized view, 81, 82
    predefined default roles, 61
    roles and users, 60

    access control models, 60
    DAC, 60
    database and application roles, 68
    dynamic data masking, 73–75
    enforcement model, 62–64
    RBAC, 60
    secondary roles, 64, 65
    using Permifrost for RBAC, 68–71
    table clustering, 81, 82
    UNDROP DATABASE, 75
    zero-copy cloning, 75–77
Snowflake connection window, 155
Snowflake DDL, 215
Snowflake ML, 191, 202
    caching, 202
    features, 201
    prediction model, 202
    workflow tools, 202
Snowflake Model Registry, 194
Snowflake's architecture
    create database, 26, 27
    create warehouse, 23–25
Snowflake services, 43
Snowflake's Feature Store, 195
Snowflakes SQL functions, 200
Snowflake's website, 20
Snowflake user interface, 18
Snowpark
    benefits, 115
    DataFrame operations, 106–109
    features, 101, 102
    machine learning integration, 112
        Base64-encoded model, 114
        binary data, 112
        libraries, 112
        linear regression, 112
        model_storage table, 113
        prediction, 114

INDEX

Snowpark (*cont.*)
    predict_linear(), 114
    scikit-learn, 112
  setting up
    get account_name, 104, 105
    current_version() function, 106
    initiate session and verify connection, 105, 106
    installation, 103
    new database, 103
    Python file, 104
  stored procedures, 110, 111
  transformative approach, 115
  UDFs, 109, 110
Snowpipe
  as AWS S3 bucket, 40
  benefits, 41
  using REST API, 40
Snowpipe auto-ingest, 42
  build data pipeline, 43, 44
  component interaction, 43
  components, 42
  configuration of Firehose, 50
  create IAM role, 51
  create new bucket for stream events, 47
  set S3 bucket notifications, 48, 49
  testing, 52
snowpipe.public.snowpipe, 46
snowpipe.public.snowstage, 46
snowpipe.public.snowtable, 46
Snowpipe REST API, 53
Snowsight, 21, 22, 27, 72
Sorting data, 176
SQL command, 27
SqlDBM tool, 147, 148, 153, 215
SQL Statement, 74, 78, 194

SRM, *see* Shared responsibility model (SRM)
Streamlit, 134
  basic Streamlit app, 136–138
  features, 134
  integration, 135
  interactive apps, 139
    connection erros, 142
    dashboard, 139
    error handling, 142
    exercise, 139–141
    query erros, 142, 143
    Streamlit erros, 142, 143
    troubleshooting, 142
  use cases, 134
Symmetric multiprocessing (SMP), 2, 3, 13
SYSADMIN role, 61

T

Tableau, 149, 154
  sheet, 157
Tableau Desktop, 146, 153, 154, 156, 158
TARGET_LAG setting, 57
Training dataset, 193

U

User-defined functions (UDFs), 86, 102, 109, 110
UTF-8, 30, 32

V

Virtual machines (VMs), 7, 10, 53, 216
Virtual private cloud (VPC), 216
Virtual warehouses (VWs), 184, 185

W, X, Y

Warehouse configuration optimization
  architectural features, 183
  cluster sizes, 183
  ETL process, 183
  scaling policies, 183

Window functions, 180, 181

Z

Zero-copy cloning, 15, 75–78

Printed in the United States
by Baker & Taylor Publisher Services